SKILLS FOR ACADEMIC SUCCESS

READING DYNAMICS

MIWAKO YAMASHINA
MITSURU YOKOYAMA
YASUKO OKINO

Reading Dynamics—Skills for Academic Success

Miwako Yamashina / Mitsuru Yokoyama / Yasuko Okino

© 2016 Cengage Learning K.K.

Adapted from *Reading for Today 4: Concepts for Today, Third Edition* published by National Geographic Learning, a part of Cengage Learning © 2011, 2004, and 1995 Cengage Learning® and *Reading for Today 5: Topics for Today, Fourth Edition* published by National Geographic Learning, a part of Cengage Learning © 2011, 2004, and 1997 Cengage Learning®

ALL RIGHTS RESERVED. No part of this work covered by the copyright herein may be reproduced, transmitted, stored or used in any form or by any means—graphic, electronic, or mechanical, including but not limited to photocopying, recording, scanning, digitizing, taping, Web distribution, information networks, or information storage and retrieval systems—without the prior written permission of the publisher.

Photo Credits:

p. 11: © David R. Frazier Photolibrary Inc./Alamy; p. 17: © Jaren Wicklund/iStockphoto.com;
p. 27: © Perkmeup/Dreamstime.com; p. 33: © Ariel Skelley/Blend Images/Jupiterimages;
p. 39: © kristian sekulic/iStockphoto.com; p. 45: © Joseph O. Holmes/portfolio.streetnine.com/Flickr/Getty Images; p. 52: © Pixland/Jupiter Images; p. 55: © Corbis/Jupiter Images;
p. 65: © image copyright bhowe 2010/Used under license from Shutterstock.com;
p. 67: © Hana/Datacraft/Alamy; p. 71: © AP Photo/Alden Pellett; p. 77: © Chris Pritchard/iStockphoto.com; p. 89: © KeithSzafranski/iStockphoto.com; p. 90: © David Boyer/National Geographic/Getty Images; p. 93: © Jim Pickerell/PhotoLibrary; p. 95: © Sam P.S. II/Alamy;
p. 97: © Comstock/Jupiter Images; p. 99: © Fuse/Thinkstock; p. 104: © AP Photo/E.J. Harris, East Oregonian

Text credits appear on page 148, which constitutes a continuation of the copyright page.

For permission to use material from this textbook or product, e-mail to **elt@cengagejapan.com**

ISBN: 978-4-86312-287-1

Cengage Learning K.K.
No. 2 Funato Building 5th Floor
1-11-11 Kudankita, Chiyoda-ku
Tokyo 102-0073
Japan

Tel: 03-3511-4392
Fax: 03-3511-4391

はしがき

　本書は『Concept for Today, 3rd edition』と『Topics for Today, 4th edition』（共に National Geographic Learning, 2011）から本文を抜粋し、日本の大学生が学習しやすいように、中・上級者向けのリーディング教材としてアレンジしたものです。『Reading Choice』、『Reading Access』、『Reading Base』の姉妹編にあたります。

　本書も「要点を把握しながら読み進める読解力を身につけるためのテキスト」というシリーズ共通のコンセプトに基づいて編集していますが、より上位レベルの学習者向けに「パラグラフごとの内容を理解する」から「少しまとまった量の英文から内容を理解する」ことに主眼を移しています。パラグラフをまたいで考える問題を増やし、自分たちで考える、あるいは推測する問題も多く採り入れました。学生が問題に自ら取り組み、答えを見つけ、すばやく情報を確認しながら段階を経て英文を読んだ後、文章全体の流れを再確認する問題を今回も準備しましたが、ここでも記述式の解答部分を多くしてあります。これらの作業を繰り返すことにより、英文を読むために必要な力が強化されることでしょう。

　英語学習において「話す」「聞く」に比べて、「読む」「書く」は地道な作業で、面白くないという印象を与えるかもしれません。けれども「読む」「書く」という作業を通して英語力を高めることで、「話す」「聞く」能力も伸ばすことができるでしょう。もちろん学習意欲を高めるためには興味深いものを読むことも大切になってきます。このテキストではどんなテーマが取り上げられているのかのぞいてみましょう。目次からキーワードを拾ってみると、「出生順」、「国際結婚」、「コンピューター」、「自尊心」、「長生き」、「天才児」、「持続可能型農業」、「動物園の使命」、「南極大陸」、「生死を分ける決断」、「新生児取り違え」、「姉妹の関係」といったものが上がってきます。これらはみな、私たちの生き方や寿命はどのようにして決まるのかや、私たちを取り巻く環境はどのように変わっていくのかなどを考える上で、ヒントになるでしょう。加えてこれらが語られる英文はテキスト用に書かれたものではなく、新聞や雑誌、あるいは一般の書籍から抜粋されたものです。リアルな話題をリアルな英語で。そしてこのテキストが少しでも皆さんの考えるヒントになれば、編著者にとって何よりの喜びです。

　今回の出版でも中嶋綾子氏、吉田剛氏をはじめとするセンゲージ ラーニングの皆さまにご尽力いただきました。シリーズ完結に際し、最後まで編著者のリクエストにお付き合いくださった皆さまに心より感謝の意を表します。

編著者一同

CONTENTS

はしがき		3
本書の構成と効果的な使い方		6
INTRODUCTION		8
UNIT 1	**LIVING IN SOCIETY**	**11**
CHAPTER 1	**The Birth-Order Myth** 出生順をめぐる神話 by Alfie Kohn, *Health*	12
CHAPTER 2	**My Husband, the Outsider** マリアンが語る国際結婚の苦労話 by Marian Hyun, *Newsday*	20
CHAPTER 3	**Hop, Skip … and Software?** コンピュータ早期導入の是非 by Victoria Irwin, *The Christian Science Monitor*	28
UNIT 2	**HEALTH AND WELL-BEING**	**39**
CHAPTER 4	**Highs and Lows in Self-Esteem** 自尊心の浮き沈み by Kim Lamb Gregory, *Scripps Howard News Service*	40
CHAPTER 5	**Who Lives Longer?** 長生きするのは誰でしょう？ by Patricia Skalka, *McCall's*	48
CHAPTER 6	**Are Gifted Children Born or Made?** 天才児は生まれつきなのか by Susan Logue, *Voice of America News*	58
UNIT 3	**THE ENVIRONMENT**	**65**
CHAPTER 7	**Students Dig into Sustainable Farming at Vermont College** 学生による持続型農業の探求：バーモント大学の場合 by Lisa Rathke, *The Associated Press*	66
CHAPTER 8	**Wilder Places for Wild Things** 動物園に託された使命とは by Sharon Begley et al., *Newsweek*	74
CHAPTER 9	**Antarctica: Whose Continent Is It Anyway?** 南極大陸：いったい誰のものなのか by Daniel and Sally Grotta, *Popular Science*	84

UNIT 4	ETHICAL ISSUES	93
CHAPTER 10	**Matters of Life and Death** 生死を分ける決断 by Dr. Francis Moore, *National Academy of Sciences*	94
CHAPTER 11	**Switched at Birth: Women Learn the Truth 56 Years Later** 新生児の取り違え：56年後の真実 by Imaeyen Ibanga, *ABC News*	102
CHAPTER 12	**Saving Her Sister's Life** 妹が姉の命を救う *Teen Vogue*	110
APPENDIX 1	FULL PASSAGE	117
APPENDIX 2	WORD LIST	143

本書の構成と効果的な使い方

本書は Introduction、4つの Unit、巻末の Appendix の2つのセクションで構成され、Unit ごとにテーマに関係する3つの Chapter、全体で12の Chapter を収録しています。各パートの特徴は次のとおりです。

INTRODUCTION

各 Chapter のタイトルと短い紹介文を掲載しています。それらの情報から Chapter の内容を予想してみましょう。実際に各 Chapter を学習した後、うまく予想できていたかどうか確認するとよいでしょう。

CHAPTER

各 Chapter は7～10ページ構成になっています。以下に、各セクションの特徴や使用例などを紹介します。

Pre-reading Preparation

Chapter のトピックに関連する選択式の設問を提示しています。各自で解答した後、ペアやクラスで話し合ってみましょう。選択肢に出てきた語句から、その Chapter の内容を予測したり、トピックについて知っていることを共有したりしましょう。また、Introduction で行った各自の予想をクラスに紹介してもよいでしょう。

Vocabulary

本文から使用頻度の高いものを重要語句として取り上げています。先生の指示に従って、事前学習として辞書で意味を調べておきましょう。授業内では本文中で使われている意味や発音を確認しましょう。日本語の意味だけでなく、英語の説明を選択肢から選んで、語句の持つニュアンスをつかみましょう。ペア活動として英語の説明を出題し合って該当する語句を答えるなど、実際に声に出してみましょう。

Reading Analysis

本文はよく知られた雑誌や新聞記事などから取ったオーセンティックな英文です。それらをパラグラフごとや複数のパラグラフからなるブロックごとに分析しながら読み進めます。本文中の表現を別の表現にパラフレーズする問題や、本文から必要な詳細を読み取って表にまとめる問題、文章の空欄に適する語句を前後の内容から推測する問題、複数のパラグラフに対して適切な見出しを付ける問題など、多面的に取り組めるよう工夫しています。また、特に難解と思われる英文は日本語に訳すことで意味を明確にし、さらに、筆者の考えや立場を問う問題によって、本文のより深い理解を目指します。

Information Organization

Reading Analysis でパラグラフやブッロクごとに確認した内容を、このセクションでは相互の関連性も意識

しながら、フローチャート、アウトライン、表のいずれかを使って情報を再度整理し、全体的な文の流れの把握を目指します。

Short Summary

Chapterの要点を再確認するために、本文を4～5行の英文で表す要約問題を設けています。空欄を埋める形式ですが、上級者は自分の言葉でサマリーを書くことにも挑戦するとよいでしょう。

Critical Thinking

Chapterの内容に関連するテーマについての英問英答です。先生の指示に従って、グループでディスカッションをしたり、自分の意見を英語でまとめたりしましょう。読んだ文章についてのアウトプット活動をすることで、内容理解が深まる効果を期待できます。

APPENDIX 1: FULL PASSAGE

各Chapterの本文全体を再掲しています。パラグラフやブロックごとの学習の後、復習として本文を通して黙読したり音読したりして、理解を確認しましょう。また、時間を測りながら音読して、WPM（Words Per Minute: 1分間に何語読めるか）を記録してみましょう。

APPENDIX 2: WORD LIST

各ChapterのVocabularyとReading Analysis内のNOTESで取り上げた重要語句の一覧です。各語句がどのChapterで使われているか調べたり、既習語と未習語を区別したりして、語彙学習に役立てましょう。

音声ファイルの無料ダウンロード ▶ http://cengage.jp/elt/Reading/

 のアイコンがある箇所の音声ファイルをダウンロードできます。

❶ 上記URLにアクセスまたはQRコードをスマートフォンなどのリーダーでスキャン（➡❹へ）
❷ 本書の表紙画像またはタイトル（Reading Dynamics）をクリック
❸ 本書のページで 音声ファイル ボタンをクリック
❹ 希望の番号をクリックして音声ファイルをダウンロード

INTRODUCTION

予測してみよう!

このテキストは12章からなっています。それぞれのタイトルと紹介文を読んで、本文の内容を予測しましょう。また、本文を読んだ後で、推測が正しかったかどうか振り返ってみましょう。

CHAPTER 1 The Birth-Order Myth

Although many people think that being the first, second, or third child in a family affects our personalities, such beliefs are really untrue.

YOUR GUESS: 解答例

> 長男・長女はしっかりしているとか、末っ子は甘えん坊とか…。出生順は本当に性格に影響を与える? 昔からいろいろ言われているけど、関係ないと思う。

CHAPTER 2 My Husband, the Outsider

A Korean family wanted their daughter to get married, but not necessarily to the man of her choice.

YOUR GUESS:

CHAPTER 3 Hop, Skip ... and Software?

Today, many young students use computers. Educators disagree on whether computer use makes these students better learners.

YOUR GUESS:

CHAPTER 4 Highs and Lows in Self-Esteem

During our lives, we experience periods of high self-esteem and low self-esteem because we are affected by biological, social, and situational factors.

YOUR GUESS:

CHAPTER 5 Who Lives Longer?

Most of us know that, on average, women live longer than men. What other factors influence how long people live?

YOUR GUESS:

CHAPTER 6 Are Gifted Children Born or Made?

Are child prodigies born or made? A reporter searches for answers to this fascinating question about gifted children.

YOUR GUESS:

CHAPTER 7 Students Dig into Sustainable Farming at Vermont College

Students at a college in Vermont get hands-on experience as they learn farming using methods that help protect the environment and raise organic crops.

YOUR GUESS:

CHAPTER 8 Wilder Places for Wild Things

Today's zoos are creating the sights and sounds of natural habitats. The animals are responding with natural behavior they never exhibited before in zoos.

YOUR GUESS:

INTRODUCTION

CHAPTER 9 Antarctica: Whose Continent Is It Anyway?

Although an international treaty helps protect the continent of Antarctica, countries still argue over who has the right to live and work there.

YOUR GUESS:

CHAPTER 10 Matters of Life and Death

A doctor offers the wisdom of his many years of experience as he discusses the controversial issue of assisted suicide.

YOUR GUESS:

CHAPTER 11 Switched at Birth: Women Learn the Truth 56 Years Later

Two women discover that the hospital where they were born 56 years earlier mistakenly gave them to the wrong mothers. They grew up in the wrong homes, without ever knowing their real families.

YOUR GUESS:

CHAPTER 12 Saving Her Sister's Life

Now a teenager, Marissa Ayala speaks about the unusual circumstances of her birth, and describes how she feels about herself and her family.

YOUR GUESS:

UNIT 1

LIVING IN SOCIETY

CHAPTER 1
The Birth-Order Myth

Pre-reading Preparation

▶ 出生順が個性や知性に影響を与えると思いますか。たとえば第一子の特徴として、どのようなイメージを持っていますか。次の中から選んでチェックしましょう（複数回答可）。

- ☐ charming
- ☐ funny
- ☐ intelligent
- ☐ kind to others
- ☐ social
- ☐ work hard
- ☐ selfish
- ☐ independent

Vocabulary

▶ 下の語句の意味を調べ、表に記入しましょう。次に、英語の説明として適切なものを枠内から選び、記号で答えましょう。

語句	意味	説明
1. promote		
2. discourage		
3. capable		
4. deserving		
5. supportive		

語句	意味	説明
6. verbal		
7. certainty		
8. motivation		
9. self-esteem		
10. competence		

a. relating to words
b. the reason for doing something or what causes someone to want to do something
c. to cause someone to lose your enthusiasm about your actions
d. to support or encourage
e. worthy of being helped or treated in a particular way
f. the ability to do something well or effectively
g. having the ability or quality necessary to do a particular thing
h. how someone feels about oneself
i. giving help, encouragement or sympathy to someone
j. the fact that is definitely true

Reading Analysis

▶ 英文を読んで、問いに答えましょう。

1

"No wonder he's so charming and funny—he's the baby of the family!" "She works hard trying to please the boss. I bet she's a firstborn." "Anyone that selfish has to be an only child."

2

It has long been ❶ <u>part of folk wisdom</u> that birth order strongly affects personality, intelligence, and achievement. ❷ <u>However, most of the research claiming that firstborns are radically different from other children has been discredited, and it now seems that any effects of birth order on intelligence or personality will likely be washed out by all the other influences in a person's life.</u> In fact, the belief in the permanent impact of birth order, according to Toni Falbo, a social psychologist at the University of Texas at Austin, "comes from the psychological theory that your personality is fixed by the time you're six. That assumption simply is incorrect."

3

The better, later, and larger studies are less likely to find birth order a useful predictor of anything. When two Swiss social scientists, Cecile Ernst and Jules Angst, reviewed 1,500 studies a few years ago, they concluded that "birth-order differences in personality ... are nonexistent in our sample. In particular, there is no evidence for a 'firstborn personality.'"

NOTES selfish「利己的な」 folk wisdom「人々の常識」 incorrect「間違った」

❶ この場合の "part of folk wisdom" の内容は何でしょうか。また、具体的にどのような事例が挙げられていますか。

内容：＿＿＿＿＿＿＿＿＿＿＿＿＿＿＿＿＿＿＿＿＿＿＿＿＿＿＿＿＿＿＿。

事例：末っ子は＿＿＿＿＿＿＿＿＿＿＿＿＿＿。長女は＿＿＿＿＿＿＿＿＿＿＿＿＿＿＿＿＿＿＿＿＿＿＿。一人っ子は＿＿＿＿＿＿＿＿＿＿＿＿＿＿＿＿＿。

❷ "However ..." で始まる文を訳しましょう。

＿＿＿＿＿＿＿＿＿＿＿＿＿＿＿＿＿＿＿＿＿＿＿＿＿＿＿＿＿＿＿＿＿＿＿＿＿
＿＿＿＿＿＿＿＿＿＿＿＿＿＿＿＿＿＿＿＿＿＿＿＿＿＿＿＿＿＿＿＿＿＿＿＿＿

❸ 社会科学者 Cecile Ernst と Jules Angst の調査について整理しましょう。

内容：改めて 1500 件の調査を行い、＿＿＿＿＿＿＿＿＿＿＿＿＿＿＿＿＿＿について調べる。

結果：＿＿＿＿＿＿＿＿＿＿＿＿＿＿＿＿＿＿＿＿＿＿＿。

UNIT 1　LIVING IN SOCIETY

❹　第1～3パラグラフの内容に合うように、次の文を完成させましょう。

On account of other influences, the effects of birth order on intelligence or personality (　　　　　　　　　　).

[　　　　　　　　　　　　　　　　　　　　]

4

1-05

　Of the early studies that seemed to show birth order mattered, most failed to recognize how other factors could confuse the issue. Take family size: Plenty of surveys showed that eldest children were overrepresented among high achievers. ❻ However, that really says less about being a firstborn than about not having many siblings, or any at all. After all, any group of firstborns is going to include a disproportionate number of children from small families, since every family has a firstborn but fewer have a fourthborn. Most experts now believe that position in the family means little when taken out of the context of *everything* going on in a particular household—whether sibling rivalry is **promoted** or **discouraged**, for instance.

5

1-06

　Parents who believe that firstborns are more **capable** or **deserving** may treat them differently, thus setting up a self-fulfilling prophecy.

NOTES　sibling「(男女の区別なく) きょうだい」　disproportionate「不釣り合いな」　rivalry「競争」　prophecy「予言」

❺　出生順が与える影響に関する研究について、第4パラグラフで指摘されている問題点は何でしょうか。それを表している文に波下線（～～）を引き、日本語で説明しましょう。

説明：_____

_____

❻　"However ..." で始まる文の内容に合うように、次の文章を完成させましょう。

According to the surveys, eldest children tend to be more successful in their achievement. But these results do not discuss much about the high achievement of (　　　　　　　　　　). Eldest children may have (　　　　　　　　　　), or they may be (　　　　　　　　　　).

❼　第5パラグラフで述べられている「第一子が自己達成的であるという予言」を生み出した要因は何であると思いますか。また、この予言はどのようにして作り上げられたと、筆者は考えていますか。

_____

_____

_____

[_____]

6

Consider the question of whether birth order affects achievement or intelligence. Many experts today suggest that birth order plays no role at all. When Judith Blake, a demographer at the University of California, Los Angeles, looked at birth patterns before 1938 and compared them to SAT scores for that group of children, she found no connection. ❾ On the other hand, (_____) does matter. "Small families are, on average, much more **supportive** of the kind of **verbal** ability that helps people succeed in school," Blake says. The reason, she believes, is that parental attention is diluted in larger families.

7

As for effects on personality, ❿ results are mixed. Research suggests that you are somewhat more likely to be outgoing, well-adjusted and independent if you grew up with few or no siblings. Two recent studies, however, found no differences on the basis of size alone. The only **certainty** is that there do not seem to be any *disadvantages* to growing up in a small family—including being an only child. After reviewing 141 studies, Falbo and a colleague found that being raised with or without siblings does not affect personality in predictable ways. Where small differences were found—such as in achievement **motivation**—they favored the only children.

NOTES demographer「人口統計学者」 SAT > Scholastic Assessment [Aptitude] Test「(米国の)大学進学適性試験」
dilute「弱める」 outgoing「社交的な」 well-adjusted「社会によく適応した」

❽ 出生順が成績や知力に影響を与えるかどうかについて、専門家はどのように考えていますか。Judith Blakeの調査結果をもとにまとめましょう。

内容：_____とSATのスコアを比較した。

結果：_____。

結論：出生順と、成績や知力とは_____。

❾ "On the other hand"のあとには、どのような文が続くと考えられますか。次の文の空欄に適する語句を入れましょう。また、そのように考えた理由も説明しましょう。

文：On the other hand, (_____) does matter.

理由：_____
_____
_____

❿ 出生順が個性に与える影響について、"results are mixed"とはどのような意味でしょうか。別の表現に書き換えて、次の文の空欄に入れましょう。また、調査結果として示されているものはどれですか。全て選びましょう。

文：As for effects on personality, (   ).

調査結果： a. Children of small families or only children are likely to be friendly, sociable, and independent.
b. Children with many siblings are more likely to be friendly, sociable and independent.
c. Only children have some disadvantages.
d. The family size alone does not affect personality.

[_____]

8

If position does not control destiny and family size has only a minor impact, what about ⓫ spacing between children? Although little research has been conducted, some psychologists believe there are more advantages to having kids far apart rather than close together. Some specialists caution that siblings close in age may be treated as a single unit.

9

This is ⓬ eyebrow-raising news, given that parents are sometimes advised not to wait too long before having a second child. However, ⓭ different studies have led to different conclusions. One found that a firstborn was more likely to have high **self-esteem** if his or her sibling was *less* than two years younger. Another indicated that spacing had no impact on social **competence**, and others note positive effects for boys but not for girls.

10

As with birth order, cautions about jumping to conclusions may be ignored by the general public. As Blake says: "You're never going to completely put to rest what people think is fun to believe."

NOTES destiny「運命」

⓫ "spacing between children"は何を意味しているでしょうか。下から1つ選びましょう。

a. How far apart children stand
b. How far apart children are in age
c. How far apart children are from their parents

CHAPTER 1　The Birth-Order Myth

⓬ "eyebrow-raising news"とはどのような意味でしょうか。また、筆者はなぜこのような表現を使ったと思いますか。その理由を考えましょう。

意味：＿＿＿＿＿＿＿＿＿＿＿＿＿＿＿＿＿＿＿ニュース

理由：＿＿＿

＿＿

＿＿

⓭ "different studies have led to different conclusions"の文が示す具体的な結論についてまとめましょう。

結論：1. きょうだいの年齢差が近いと＿＿＿＿＿＿＿＿＿＿＿＿＿＿＿＿＿＿＿＿＿＿。

　　　2. きょうだいの年齢差は＿＿＿＿＿＿＿＿＿＿＿＿＿＿＿＿＿＿＿＿＿＿＿。

　　　3. 男女を比べると＿＿＿＿＿＿＿＿＿＿＿＿＿＿＿＿＿＿＿＿＿＿＿＿＿＿＿。

⓮ 第10パラグラフで引用されたJudith Blakeのコメントはどのような意味でしょうか。また、筆者はなぜこのコメントを引用したのだと思いますか。その理由を考えましょう。

意味：＿＿＿＿＿＿＿＿＿＿＿＿＿＿＿＿＿＿＿＿＿＿＿＿＿＿＿＿＿＿＿＿＿＿＿＿＿＿＿

理由：＿＿＿＿＿＿＿＿＿＿＿＿＿＿＿＿＿＿＿＿＿＿＿＿＿＿＿＿＿＿＿＿＿＿＿＿＿＿＿

＿＿

＿＿

⓯ それぞれのブロック（4と5、6と7、8〜10）の内容にふさわしい見出しを下から選んで、[　]に記入しましょう。

- Do Kids Need More Space?
- Old Theories Die Hard
- Putting Birth Order in Context

UNIT 1   LIVING IN SOCIETY

Information Organization

▶ 下のアウトラインを使って、本文の内容を整理しましょう。空欄にあてはまる語を英語で記入しましょう。空欄に入る語は1語とは限りません。

I. The Myth and the Reality about Birth Order
  A. The myth: Birth order (1.   ) personality, intelligence, and achievement.
  B. The reality: This myth is (2.   ).

II. The Findings of Studies on Birth Order, Personality, and Intelligence
  A. The findings of Cecile Ernst and Jules Angst
    • Birth-Order differences in personality are (3.   ).
    • There is (4.   ) for a firstborn personality.
  B. The findings of Judith Blake
    • Birth order (5.   ) intelligence; she looked at birth patterns before 1938 and compared them to SAT scores for that group of children, and she found (6.   ).

III. Other Factors Affecting Personality and Intelligence
  A. Parents expectations
    • Parents who believe that (7.   ) may treat them differently, thus setting up a self-fulfilling prophecy.
  B. Numbers of siblings
    • It does affect (8.   ); small families tend to be (9.   ) of the kind of verbal ability that helps people succeed in school.
  C. Spacing between siblings
    • Some psychologists believe there are more advantages to (10.   ).

IV. Conflicting Research Regarding Family Size and Personality
  A. You are more likely to be outgoing, well-adjusted, and independent if you grew up (11.   ).
  B. Two studies found no differences on the basis of (12.   ).
  C. One study found that a firstborn was more likely to have good self-esteem if his or her sibling was less than two years younger.
  D. One study indicated that spacing had (13.   ) on social competence.
  E. Other studies note positive effects for boys but not for girls.

Short Summary

▶ 空欄に適する単語を記入して、本文全体の要約文を完成させましょう。

Hundreds of studies have been done on the effects of birth order on (1.), (2.) and (3.). Because many of the studies came up with (4.) results, it seems that the effect of birth order on these factors is a (5.).

Critical Thinking

▶ 以下の質問について自分の意見をまとめましょう。そして、ペアやグループで話し合ったり、クラスで発表したりしましょう。

1. According to the article, the number of siblings a person has affects his or her personality. Judith Blake says, "Small families are, on average, much more supportive of the kind of verbal ability that helps people succeed in school." The reason, she believes, is that parental attention is diluted in larger families. Why do you think parental attention might be diluted in larger families? Do you agree with this theory? Explain your answer.

2. The studies that the author refers to in this article came up with very different results. How do you think we might explain these different findings?

CHAPTER 2

My Husband, the Outsider

Pre-reading Preparation

▶ あなたが結婚する場合、結婚相手の条件として家族が大切だと考えるのはどのような点でしょうか。次の中から選んでチェックしましょう（複数回答可）。

- ☐ academic background
- ☐ age
- ☐ class
- ☐ his/her family
- ☐ marital history
- ☐ income
- ☐ race
- ☐ religion

Vocabulary

▶ 下の語句の意味を調べ、表に記入しましょう。次に、英語の説明として適切なものを枠内から選び、記号で答えましょう。

語句	意味	説明	語句	意味	説明
1. religious			6. reluctantly		
2. relative			7. appreciate		
3. insulting			8. persistence		
4. acknowledge			9. generous		
5. delightful			10. elaborate		

a. to admit or accept that something is true or that a situation exists
b. to understand or enjoy the good qualities or value of someone or something
c. very nice and pleasant
d. carefully planned and produced with many details
e. larger or more than the usual or expected amount
f. very impolite or offensive to someone, and showing a lack of respect
g. continuing to exist or happen, often for longer than is usual or desirable
h. a member of your family
i. relating to religion in general or to a particular religion
j. slowly and unwillingly

Reading Analysis

▶ 英文を読んで、問いに答えましょう。

1

When my husband-to-be and I announced our engagement, ❶ <u>people were curious about the kind of wedding we would have</u>. He is an Irish-Ukrainian from the Bronx, and a lapsed Catholic, while I am an American-born Korean from New Jersey. Some of my husband's friends must have been expecting an exotic wedding ceremony.

2

We disappointed many people. Far from being exotic, or even very **religious**, our ceremony was performed in English by a Unitarian minister on a hotel balcony. But when my husband and I decided to have 50 guests instead of 150, we ❸ <u>caused an uproar</u> among **relatives** and family friends, especially on the Korean side.

3

"It's very embarrassing," my father complained. "Everyone wants to know why you won't listen to me and invite the people you should."

"Well, whose wedding is this, anyway?" I asked.

NOTES lapsed「時代遅れの」 Unitarian「ユニタリアン派の（キリスト教の宗派の一つ）」 uproar「大騒ぎ」

❶ なぜ下線部❶のように感じたのでしょうか。具体的に説明しましょう。

二人がそれぞれ＿＿＿＿＿＿＿＿＿＿＿＿＿＿＿＿＿＿＿＿＿＿＿＿＿＿

結婚だったので、＿＿＿＿＿＿＿＿＿＿＿＿＿＿＿＿＿＿＿＿＿＿＿＿＿と期待したから。

❷ 下線部❶の思いは叶えられたのでしょうか。[ ]内の正しいほうを○で囲み、それがわかる語句を書き出しましょう。また、そうなった理由を考えましょう。

[Yes / No]　　語句：＿＿＿＿＿＿＿＿＿＿＿＿＿＿＿

理由：＿＿＿＿＿＿＿＿＿＿＿＿＿＿＿＿＿＿＿＿＿＿＿＿＿＿＿＿＿

❸ "caused an uproar" はどのようなことを意味していますか。最も適切なものを選びましょう。また、このようなことになった理由を簡潔にまとめましょう。

　a. Relatives and family friends were very happy.
　b. Relatives and family friends were very disturbed.
　c. Relatives and family friends were disagreed.

理由：＿＿＿＿＿＿＿＿＿＿＿＿＿＿＿＿＿＿＿＿＿＿＿＿＿＿＿＿＿

4
🎧 1-15

④ <u>What a dumb question</u>. I had forgotten for a moment that I was dealing with Koreans. It was bad enough that I had decided to marry a non-Korean, but highly **insulting** that I was not giving everyone the chance to snicker over it in person. I found out after the wedding that my father was asked, "How does it feel to have an American son-in-law?"

"My son-in-law is a good man," he said. "Better to have a good American son-in-law than a bad Korean one."

5
🎧 1-16

He had not always felt that way. For years, he ignored the non-Koreans I was dating—it took him about a year to remember my husband's name. But when I was a freshman in college, I dated my father's dream of a son-in-law, David, an American-born Korean from a respected family, who was doing brilliantly at Harvard and had plans for law school. When the relationship ended, my father preferred not to **acknowledge** the fact.

6
🎧 1-17

⑤ <u>When it became clear that David would never be his son-in-law, my father started dropping hints at the dinner table about some handsome and **delightful** young doctor working for him, who was right off the plane from Seoul—there seemed to be a steady supply.</u> This started during my senior year in college, and continued until sometime after my engagement.

NOTES dumb「ばかな、愚かな」 snicker「にやにや笑う」 son-in-law「娘むこ」

❹ "What a dumb question."とは、どのような問いかけでしょうか。また、どのようなことが馬鹿げているのか考えましょう。

- ■ _____ことを忘れ、_____
  _____父に対して発した問いかけ。
- ■韓国人と_____ばかりか、それを_____
  ことは、とても_____だと思い至らなかったこと。

❺ 筆者マリアン(Marian)の父が娘の結婚相手についてどのように考えていたのかまとめましょう。また、Davidと別れて以降については下線部を訳しましょう。

韓国人ではないデートの相手：_____

理想の相手としての具体的人物：_____生まれの韓国人David。ハーバード大学の学生で、_____予定。

Davidと別れて以降（下線部訳）：_____
_____
_____
_____

❻ 最終的にマリアンの父は、どのような考えになったでしょうか。

7
1-18

The one time I did go out with a Korean doctor was at my mother's request. "Please, just once," she said. "One of my college friends has a son who wants to get married, and she thought of you."

"You expect me to go out with a guy who lets his mommy pick his dates?" I asked.

"He's very ❼ traditional," she explained. "If you refuse to meet him, my friend will think I'm too snobby to want her son in our family. I'll lose face."

8
1-19

"OK, just this once," I said **reluctantly**. A few days later, I sat in an Indian restaurant with the Korean doctor. After several start-and-stop attempts at conversation, the doctor told me I should live in Korea for a while.

9
1-20

"Korea is a great country," he said. "I think you ought to **appreciate** it more. And you should learn to speak Korean. I don't understand why you can't speak your native language."

"English is my native language," I said. "I wish I could speak Korean, but I don't have the time to learn it now."

"You are Korean," he insisted. "You should speak your mother tongue." A mouthful of food kept me from saying more than "Mmmm," but I found myself stabbing my tandoori chicken with remarkable violence.

10
1-21

Despite our obvious ❾ incompatibility, the doctor kept asking me out. For weeks, I had to turn down invitations to dinner, movies and concerts—even rides to visit my parents—before he finally stopped calling.

NOTES stab「…を突き刺す」 incompatibility「相容れないもの、不一致」

❼ 見合い相手をマリアンの母は "traditional" と評していますが、ここでの "traditional" はどのような人物を意味していると思いますか。

❽ 次の質問の答えとして、最も適切なものを選びましょう。

Why was the author stabbing her tandoori chicken with remarkable violence?
 a. She didn't like the food.
 b. She wasn't hungry.
 c. She was angry at the Korean doctor.

UNIT 1   LIVING IN SOCIETY

❾ "incompatibility" はどのようなことを意味しますか。[　]内の正しいほうを○で囲み、英文を完成させましょう。また、それがわかる具体例を日本語で述べましょう。

Marian and the doctor [got along / did not get along] well because they [had / didn't have] anything in common.

具体例：＿＿＿＿＿＿＿＿＿＿＿＿＿＿＿＿＿＿＿＿＿＿＿＿＿＿＿＿＿＿＿＿＿＿＿＿＿＿＿

11
1-22

During a visit to Seoul a few years later, I realized that this kind of ❿ <u>dogged persistence</u> during ⓫ <u>Korean courtship</u> was quite common. In fact, my own father had used it successfully. My mother told me he proposed to her the day after they were introduced at a dinner given by matchmaking friends. She told him he was crazy when she turned him down. Undaunted, he (　　　　　) her for three months until she finally gave in.

12
1-23

My parents have now been married for almost 40 years, but what worked for them was not about to work for me. I think one reason my father did not object to having a non-Korean son-in-law—aside from actually liking my husband—was that he was relieved to have one ⓬ <u>at all</u>.

When I was 24, he started asking me, "When are you going to make me a grandfather?"

13
1-24

And when I turned 25, the age when unmarried women in Korea are considered old maids, my other relatives expressed their concern.

"You better hurry up and meet someone," one of my aunts told me. "Do you have a boyfriend?"

"Yes," I said …. I had met my future husband a few months earlier in an office where I was working as a temporary secretary.

"Is he Korean?" she asked.

"No." My aunt considered this for a moment, then said, "You better hurry up and meet someone. Do you want me to help?"

NOTES   matchmaking「結婚仲介」　undaunted「ひるみもしないで」

❿ マリアンは自分の父が母に対して取った行動を "dogged persistence" のようなものだったと考えています。父の行動を表す動詞として最も適切なものを下から選び、本文中の空欄に入れましょう。

[caught / hounded / ran / walked]

⓫ "Korean courtship" とは、どのようなことか考えましょう。

求愛の際、＿＿＿＿＿＿＿＿＿＿＿＿＿＿＿＿＿＿＿＿＿＿＿＿＿＿こと。

24

❷ "at all" の意味を考えましょう。

_____

❸ 第 13 パラグラフは何を説明するための段落でしょうか。

早く結婚相手を決めないと、_____ からいろいろ言われるので、父はマリアンが _____ を、たとえその人が _____ でないにしても、決めてくれて _____ ということを強調するため。

14

My husband saved me from spinsterhood. Just barely, in some eyes—I was married at 26. We received **generous** gifts, many from people who had not been invited to the wedding. This convinced my father more than ever that we should have invited all of his friends and relatives. He felt this way for several years, until one of my sisters got engaged and made **elaborate** plans to feed and entertain 125 wedding guests.

15

As the expenses mounted, my father took me aside and asked me to talk to my sister.

"Tell her she should have a small simple wedding," he said. "Like yours."

NOTES spinsterhood「未婚の状態、独身」

❹ マリアンの結婚が決まったときのマリアンの思いと父の思いとを比べてみましょう。

マリアン：_____ という気持ち。これは _____ という語句からわかる。

父：親類縁者のみんなを式に _____ ことを _____ と思っている。これは _____ という語を使うことにより強調される。

❺ 父の気持ちが変わるきっかけになったできごとと、どのように変わったかを考えましょう。また、その変化がわかる部分に下線を引きましょう。

できごと：_____

変化した気持ち：_____

UNIT 1 LIVING IN SOCIETY

Information Organization

▶ 下の表を使って、本文の内容を整理しましょう。空欄にあてはまる語を英語で記入し、マリアンの結婚について、それぞれの人の意見をまとめましょう。空欄に入る語は1語とは限りません。

Person	How does this person feel about Marian and the marriage?
Marian	She wanted to marry a man of her own (1.). She did not want to marry a (2.) Korean man.
Marian's father	He wanted her to marry a (3.) man. When she was 24, he wanted her to (4.). He wanted her to have a big wedding so he could invite many (5.).
Marian's (6.)	She wanted her to marry a Korean man. She wanted to help Marian choose a (7.) man. She wanted to help Marian choose a husband.
Marian's (8.)	She wanted her to marry a Korean man. She wanted her to get married before she became (9.). She didn't acknowledge that Marian was (10.) a non-Korean man.
The Korean doctor	He seemed to feel that Marian should behave as a (11.) Korean and follow Korean (12.).
Marian's husband	Marian (13.) give us any information about her husband's (14.).

Short Summary

▶ 空欄に適する単語を記入して、本文全体の要約文を完成させましょう。

Marian describes her experiences with her family as she dated and got (¹.   ). As an (².   ) Korean, she had many (³.   ) conflicts with her parents, other relatives, and the Korean men she dated. In the end, she married a (⁴.   ) man and had a (⁵.   ) wedding.

Critical Thinking

▶ 以下の質問について自分の意見をまとめましょう。そして、ペアやグループで話し合ったり、クラスで発表したりしましょう。

1. Marian expresses her opinion and describes how her mother and father feel. However, she does not discuss her husband's point of view. Why do you think she decided not to write about his opinion?

2. What is the author's tone? For example, is the writing humorous, serious, sarcastic, etc.? What makes you think so?

CHAPTER 3

Hop, Skip … and Software?

Pre-reading Preparation

▶ 小学校でコンピュータを導入する場合、どのような利用が効果的と考えますか。次の中から選んでチェックしましょう（複数回答可）。

- ☐ blog writing
- ☐ educational games
- ☐ e-mail
- ☐ graphic drawing
- ☐ Internet search
- ☐ programming
- ☐ video phone

Vocabulary

▶ 下の語句の意味を調べ、表に記入しましょう。次に、英語の説明として適切なものを枠内から選び、記号で答えましょう。

語句	意味	説明
1. exception		
2. embrace		
3. enthusiast		
4. virtually		
5. outperform		

語句	意味	説明
6. relevant (to)		
7. facilitate		
8. integrate		
9. vital		
10. oversee		

a. closely connected or appropriate to the matter in hand
b. a person who is very interested in a particular activity or subject
c. a particular thing or situation that is not included in a general statement
d. to combine one thing with another so that the two things become linked
e. to do better than; to be more successful than
f. to accept something and start supporting something
g. to make sure that a job or an activity is done properly
h. necessary or very important
i. to make something easier to happen
j. in practical terms; nearly; almost

Reading Analysis

▶ 英文を読んで、問いに答えましょう。

1

Jody Spanglet's seventh- and eighth-grade students at Charlottesville Waldorf School in Virginia are studying revolutions. They dissect the Declaration of Independence, delve into the French rebellion against Louis XIV, and read about the various inventors who sparked the Industrial Revolution. But this study happens to be profoundly counterrevolutionary in today's cyber age: Not a single classroom in the school—from kindergarten through eighth grade—contains a computer.

2

Contrast that with the B.F. Yancey Elementary School in the southwest corner of the same county, Albemarle, in central Virginia. Here, computers are considered a rich resource and are used everywhere, from kindergarten through fifth grade. Third graders working on oral history projects, for example, must first pass an online minicourse. They can then take home digital video cameras and download their oral history interviews onto the school computers, which are later made available on the school's website.

NOTES dissect「…を詳細に調べる」 delve into …「…を徹底的に調べる」
Louis XIV「ルイ14世：1643～1715年に在位したフランス国王」 profoundly「まったく」
counterrevolutionary「反革命的な」 cyber age「サイバー時代」
Albemarle「アルベマール：米国バージニア州中央部に位置する郡」

❶ 空欄に適語を入れて、Charlottesville Waldorf School と B.F. Yancey Elementary School の相違についてまとめましょう。

Both schools are in the same (　　　　　　). There are no (　　　　　　) at the Charlottesville Waldorf School. In contrast, computers are considered a rich (　　　　　　) and are used (　　　　　　) at the B.F. Yancey Elementary School.

❷ B.F. Yancey Elementary School の3年生の授業活動の具体例をまとめましょう。

口述歴史記録プロジェクトに取り組むために、まず＿＿＿＿＿＿＿に合格しなければならない。その後、＿＿＿＿＿＿＿を自宅に持ち帰り、口述歴史インタビューを録画する。後にそれを学校のコンピュータに＿＿＿＿＿＿＿する。

3 ❸ While the computerless Waldorf School is an **exception** in a nation that tends to **embrace** the technology revolution, both schools find themselves on the cutting edge of a debate about if and how computers should be introduced to children at the elementary school level. At one end of the spectrum are coalitions such as the Alliance for Childhood, which has called for a moratorium on computers for students in early childhood and elementary schools. Concerns range from health issues to the need for stronger bonds between children and adults and more hands-on, active play in learning. At the other end are educators and technology **enthusiasts**, who believe that the use of computers at an early age—even when led by an adult—can open a child's mind to ideas and concepts that will kindle a great desire for learning, and perhaps make a child "smarter." Parents and guardians stand somewhere in the middle.

4 Many parents, who brag that their not-yet-three-year-old can type his or her name on a keyboard to enter a computer game, also admit to a grudging guilt that they did not instead send that same toddler outdoors to explore the wonders of blooming crocuses peeking through a layer of snow. "I don't think an elementary school **virtually** devoid of technology is necessarily bad," says Gene Maeroff, a professor at Columbia University's Teachers College and the author of "A Classroom of One: How Online Learning Is Changing Our Schools and Colleges." "Nor do I think a school loaded with technology is necessarily good, or better, at meeting students' needs," he says. "Computers can enhance education. But those possibilities become greater as kids get older, particularly at the secondary level and absolutely at the college or postgraduate level."

5 Various studies show different effects of computer use in the classroom. In the late 1990s, the Educational Testing Service found that middle school students with well-trained teachers who used computers for "simulations and applications" in math class **outperformed** students on standardized tests who had not used them for that purpose. Meanwhile, eighth graders whose teachers used computers primarily for "drill and practice" performed even worse.

NOTES on the cutting edge of ...「…の最前線で」 spectrum「範囲、(比喩的に) 様々な意見」 coalition「連合体」
moratorium「一時停止、延期」 kindle「…をかき立てる」 guardian「保護者」 grudging「しぶしぶの」
crocus「クロッカス (植物の名称)」 devoid of ...「…を欠いている」
the Educational Testing Service「ETS：TOEIC や TOEFL などを開発している米国のテスト開発機関」
standardized test「標準テスト」

❸ "While ..." で始まる文を訳しましょう。

_____
_____
_____
_____

❹ コンピュータ導入に関する様々な立場について、まとめましょう。

立場	人・団体	意見
反対	_____ _____	幼児教育や小学校でのコンピュータの_____を求める。懸念事項は、_____から人との結びつきや、より実践的な学習の_____まで様々ある。
中立	_____	
賛成	テクノロジー推進派	コンピュータを早期に使用することによって、_____ _____ような発想に子どもたちが心を開き、その子どもたちが_____なる可能性がある。

❺ Gene Maeroff 教授の発言を整理しましょう。

「テクノロジーを導入していない小学校が必ずしも_____と思わないし、テクノロジーをフル装備している学校がよりうまく生徒のニーズに_____とも思わないが、コンピュータは教育を_____。ただし、その可能性は年齢が高くなるほど、_____だろう」

❻ 第5パラグラフの内容を表す英文として、最も適切なものを選びましょう。

a. Some studies found that middle school students who used computers for "drill and practice" did better on standardized tests than students who did not use them for that purpose.
b. Some studies show that students who use computers do better on standardized tests than students who do not use computers in class. Other studies show the opposite results.
c. Some studies show that eighth graders who used computers for "drill and practice" did better on standardized tests than students who did not use them for that purpose.

Born Digital

6

Computer technology is a fact of life in U.S. schools and homes. Currently, 98 percent of public schools have access to the Internet in their schools. And one in five students in public schools overall have access to a computer. In urban schools, that number drops to one in nine—which one technology advocate calls "not a digital divide, but a digital chasm." Today, according to the National Center for Educational Statistics, 80 percent of eighth graders have access to a computer at home. Despite tightened state budgets, efforts are under way throughout the country to make technology even more **relevant to** students and learning. In Maine, every single seventh grader (of whom there are slightly more than 18,000) has a laptop computer. In April, the state will begin sending computers to all eighth graders, too. At Walton Middle School in Charlottesville, Virginia, seventh graders are using what some predict will be the educational technology of the future—❽ (　　　)—to **facilitate** writing.

7

But how computers are used varies greatly. Elliot Soloway, of the University of Michigan's Center for Highly Interactive Computing in Education, surveyed 4,000 schools last year and found that 65 percent of students in public schools, including high schools, spend less than 15 minutes a week using computers to access the Internet. *PC Magazine* reports that, of the $5 billion spent in the past decade to get computers into schools, 17 percent was used to educate teachers how to use the computers and **integrate** them into the curriculum. That gets to the heart of a ❿ **debate** over whether computer use in school is beneficial to students—or merely expensive window dressing.

8

Quality teachers have always worked toward finding many different paths to build basic knowledge and skills that students will need to succeed in school and life, says Becky Fisher, assistant director of the Department of Technology for the Albemarle County Schools. "Adding technology to the mix only makes a great teacher even better," she says. "The issue is not whether technology is appropriate for students—most kindergartners have already mastered more technology than existed when I was a child. Rather, it is whether our teachers are supported in a way to maximize the benefits of technology."

 born digital「ボーンデジタル：最初からデジタルデータで制作されるコンテンツ」 fact of life「日常よくあること」
digital divide「デジタル・ディバイド、情報格差」 chasm「亀裂」
the National Center for Educational Statistics「全国教育統計センター」 window dressing「うわべだけのお飾り」

❼ 第6パラグラフの下線で示した数値はそれぞれ何を示しているか説明しましょう。また、（　）には数字を記入しましょう。

98%：＿＿＿＿＿＿＿＿＿＿＿＿＿＿＿＿＿＿＿＿＿＿＿＿＿＿＿できる割合

one in five =（　　）%：＿＿＿＿＿＿＿＿＿＿＿＿＿＿＿コンピュータにアクセスできる割合

one in nine =（　　）%：＿＿＿＿＿＿＿＿＿＿＿＿＿＿＿コンピュータにアクセスできる割合

80%：＿＿＿＿＿＿＿＿＿＿＿＿＿＿＿＿＿＿＿＿＿＿＿＿＿＿＿の割合

every single =（　　）%：＿＿＿＿＿＿＿＿＿＿＿＿＿＿＿＿＿＿＿＿＿＿＿＿＿の割合

❽ 本文中の空欄に最も適する語句を下から選び、○で囲みましょう。

［ TVs / desktop computers / handheld computers / cell phones ］

❾ Elliot Solowayの調査結果をまとめましょう。

調査数：＿＿＿＿校
結果：高校を含む公立学校の生徒の＿＿＿＿%は、＿＿＿＿＿＿＿＿＿＿＿＿＿しかコンピュータを使ってインターネットにアクセスしなかった。

❿ "debate"の内容を答えましょう。

過去10年で学校にコンピュータを導入するため＿＿＿＿ドル費やされているが、学校におけるコンピュータ使用が＿＿＿＿＿＿＿＿＿＿＿＿＿＿＿のか、ただの＿＿＿＿＿＿＿＿＿＿にすぎないのかの議論。

⓫ テクノロジー導入について、Becky Fisherが重要だと考えていることをまとめましょう。

問題はテクノロジーが生徒に＿＿＿＿＿＿＿＿＿＿＿＿ではなく、テクノロジーの恩恵を最大限に活かすことができるように＿＿＿＿＿＿＿＿＿＿＿＿＿＿＿＿＿＿かどうかである。

UNIT 1 LIVING IN SOCIETY

[_____]

9
1-35

Those who think technology in the classroom should wait see technology differently. "We strongly believe that ⑫<u>actual experience</u> is **vital** for young children," says Jody Spanglet of the Waldorf School in Charlottesville. "It is important for students to interact with one another, with teachers, and with the world—to explore ideas, participate in the creative process, and develop their knowledge, skills, abilities, and inner qualities." Nancy Regan, an administrator at the school, says: "A computer is a mediated experience. You touch the keyboard, but what happens online is not your doing. Our whole curriculum is based on human connection."

10
1-36

It is not that the Waldorf School eschews technology. For example, it has a website. And Ms. Regan says computers at the high school level are a good idea. Her seventh and eighth graders will soon be doing a report on inventors from the Industrial Revolution. To do so, they are required to use at least three resources, one of which can be the Internet. Kim McCormick, who has two daughters, ages five and eight, at the Charlottesville Waldorf School says her family is not the least bit uncomfortable that their children's classrooms have no instructional computers. "We want them to get to know the world on a firsthand basis," says Ms. McCormick, a public school teacher. Her husband is a computer program analyst. "They see us using computers for work. But we don't have any kids' things on our computer. I have looked up butterflies for them before, so they know it can be a tool and resource. But they will learn to use a computer so quickly later. My husband, who works with computers for a living, didn't learn those skills until after college."

NOTES　mediated「媒介の」　eschew「…を避ける」

⑫ "actual experience"の具体的な内容を述べている箇所に波下線（ ～～ ）を引き、その内容を日本語で答えましょう。

内容：＿＿＿＿＿＿＿＿＿＿＿＿＿＿＿＿＿＿＿＿＿＿＿＿＿＿＿＿＿＿＿＿＿＿＿＿＿＿

⑬ このブロック（**9**と**10**）の内容に最もふさわしい見出しを下から選んで、[ ]に記入しましょう。

- The Human Connection
- Instructional Computers
- A Computer Program

Going Online, Bit By Bit

11 Technology enthusiasts say computers should be introduced in stages. Paula White is a resource teacher for gifted students who helps integrate technology into the classroom at Yancey. White says that, at Yancey, while even kindergartners are using computers in the classroom—to count candy hearts on Valentine's Day, for instance—the teacher is the one entering the information. It is not as though children at Yancey are being plunked in front of a machine without interacting with teachers. But at some schools, lack of interaction is a real concern. A mother of three children in another Virginia elementary school says ⑭ <u>she is disappointed</u> in the use of computers in two of her children's classes. When they get computer time, it is usually in the morning or late afternoon, she says, when a teacher wants to grab some extra time at his or her desk.

12 Bette Manchester of the Maine Learning Technology Initiative, which **oversees** the state's laptop project, says even the best teachers have a hard time incorporating the four or five desk computers that often sit in elementary classrooms. One-to-one computer access changes everything. "We've made this crystal clear: This is not about technology or software, it is about teaching kids," Ms. Manchester says. The success of the Maine program, she notes, depends heavily on leadership among teachers in the state, as well as the complete integration of laptops into every school's curriculum. Training involves teachers, staff, students, and parents, and started well before the computers arrived. Manchester says middle school is a great time to give students intimate access to the technology. ⑯ "<u>They are at a critical stage developmentally</u>," she says. "These kids are learning how to learn, not simply reading to learn anymore. It's been very exciting watching them take off."

NOTES candy heart「ハート形のキャンディー」 plunk「…を放り出す」 intimate「密接な」 developmentally「発達的に」

⑭ "she is disappointed" の理由として、最も適切なものを選びましょう。

　a. Her children use computers in their classrooms too much.
　a. Her children never use computers in school.
　c. The teachers do not help her children use computers in school.

⑮ メイン州でのPCプロジェクトの成功の要因は何でしょうか。Bette Manchester の考えについてまとめましょう。

メイン州の教員たちの＿＿＿＿＿＿＿とノートパソコンを各学校の＿＿＿＿＿＿＿＿＿＿＿＿＿＿＿＿＿＿＿が大きい。トレーニングには、教員、スタッフ、生徒、そして親たちが全員関与し、それはコンピュータが実際に＿＿＿＿＿＿＿＿＿＿＿＿から始まった。

❶ "They are at a critical stage developmentally"を他の表現で言い換えている箇所に波下線を引き、その意味を日本語で答えましょう。

意味：_____

Information Organization

▶ 下の表を使って、本文の内容を整理しましょう。空欄にあてはまる語を英語で記入して、教室へのコンピュータ導入に関する各組織の意見を完成させ、支持（Support）か反対（Oppose）か、どちらか正しいほうの立場を○で囲みましょう。

Organization	Opinion
Charlottesville Waldorf School	They believe actual experience is (1.) for young children. "It is important for students to interact with one another, with teachers, and with the world—to explore ideas, (2.) in the creative process, and develop their knowledge, skills, abilities, and inner qualities. [Support / Oppose]
B.F. Yancey Elementary School	Students at Yancey (3.) with teachers as well as with computers. Even kindergartners are using computers in the classroom. [Support / Oppose]
The Alliance for Childhood	They call for a moratorium on computers for students in (4.) schools. Concerns range from health issues to the need for stronger (5.) between children and adults. [Support / Oppose]
Columbia University's Teachers College	"Computers can (6.) education. But those possibilities become greater as kids get older, particularly at the secondary level…." [Support / Oppose]
Educational Testing Service	They found that middle school students with (7.) teachers who used computers for "simulation and applications" in math class (8.) students on standardized tests who had not used them for that purpose. [Support (if used correctly) / Oppose]

CHAPTER 3　Hop, Skip … and Software?

Department of Technology for the Albemarle County Schools	"Adding technology to the mix only makes a great teacher even (⁹.). The issue is not whether technology is appropriate for students…. Rather, it is whether our teachers are supported in a way to (¹⁰.) the benefits of technology." ［ Support / Oppose ］
Maine Learning Technology Initiative	The success of the program depends heavily on (¹¹.) among teachers in the state, as well as the complete (¹².) of laptops into every school's curriculum. ［ Support / Oppose ］

Short Summary

▶ 空欄に適する単語を記入して、本文全体の要約文を完成させましょう。

There is a current (¹.   ) about whether to introduce computers to (².   ) school children. Some educators believe that children need more hands-on, (³.   ) play in learning, while others believe that the use of (⁴.   ) at a young age can stimulate a strong (⁵.   ) to learn.

Critical Thinking

▶ 以下の質問について自分の意見をまとめましょう。そして、ペアやグループで話し合ったり、クラスで発表したりしましょう。

1. The Alliance for Childhood cites health concerns as one reason why young students should not have computers in the classroom. What might these health concerns be?

2. Read Paragraph 5 again. This paragraph states, "Various studies show different effects of computer use in the classroom." According to this paragraph, what factor can determine how useful computers are in the classroom?

UNIT 2
HEALTH AND WELL-BEING

CHAPTER 4

Highs and Lows in Self-Esteem

Pre-reading Preparation

▶ あなたはself-で始まる単語をどのくらい知っていますか。次の中から意味を知っているものをチェックしましょう（複数回答可）。また、他にどのような単語がありますか。

- ☐ self-approval
- ☐ self-doubt
- ☐ self-esteem
- ☐ self-help
- ☐ self-love
- ☐ self-regard
- ☐ self-sacrifice
- ☐ self-satisfaction

Vocabulary

▶ 下の語句の意味を調べ、表に記入しましょう。次に、英語の説明として適切なものを枠内から選び、記号で答えましょう。

語句	意味	説明	語句	意味	説明
1. plunge			6. overall		
2. launch			7. coincide		
3. similarity			8. continuity		
4. transition			9. chaos		
5. feedback			10. vulnerable		

- a. the process in which something changes from one state to another
- b. to start or set in motion
- c. to happen at the same time
- d. to bring into a specified condition or state suddenly
- e. the state of complete disorder and confusion
- f. information about reactions to a product, a person's performance of a task, etc.
- g. weak and without protection; easily hurt physically or emotionally
- h. taking everything into account
- i. the state or fact of having a resemblance in appearance, character, or quantity
- j. the unbroken and consistent existence or operation of something over time

Reading Analysis

▶ 英文を読んで、問いに答えましょう。

1

No one in the Gould family of Westlake Village, California, was surprised by a study suggesting a person's age and stage of life may have a bigger impact on self-esteem than we ever realized. ❷ A study of about 350,000 people likens a person's self-esteem across the human lifespan to a roller coaster ride, starting with an inflated sense of self-approval in late childhood that **plunges** in adolescence. Self-esteem rises steadily through adulthood, only to drop to its lowest point ever in old age. "I've gone through pretty much all of those cycles," Fred Gould said. At 60, he is edging toward retirement. Fred's wife, Eileen, 46, is a businesswoman in the throes of mid-adulthood and, according to the study, predisposed to a healthy self-regard. At 21, the Goulds' son, Jeff, has just **launched** that heady climb into adulthood and a buoyant self-regard after an adolescence fraught with the usual perils of self-doubt and hormonal warfare. His sister, Aly, 17, disagrees with a lot of the study, believing instead that each individual has an intrinsic sense of self-esteem that remains relatively constant. But she does agree that adolescence can give even the most solid sense of self-esteem a sound battering. "As a teenager, I can definitely speak for all of us when I say we bag on ourselves," Aly said.

NOTES liken ... to ~「…を~にたとえる」 lifespan「生涯」 self-approval「自己是認」 adolescence「思春期」 throe「苦悩」
be predisposed to ...「…へと向かう傾向がある」 self-regard「自己愛」 heady「性急な」 buoyant「快活な、楽天的な」
fraught with ...「…に満ちた」 peril「危険」 self-doubt「自己疑念」 hormonal「ホルモンの」 warfare「闘争」
intrinsic「本来備わっている」 battering「ひどい打撃」 bag on ...「…を非難する」

❶ 第1パラグラフの主旨に合うように、次の文章を完成させましょう。

The author compares the changes in a person's (　　　　　　) over a lifetime to a (　　　　　　) ride. It begins high, then gets (　　　　　　) and higher throughout a person's life.

❷ "A study ..."で始まる文を訳しましょう。

_____

_____

_____

❸ Gould 家の家族の状況を整理しましょう。

Fred：60 歳。＿＿＿＿＿が近づいている。

Eileen：＿＿歳のビジネスウーマン。成人期の苦闘の真っ只中で、健全な＿＿＿＿＿を持ちやすい時期。

Jeff：＿＿歳。思春期から成人期にさしかかったところ。楽天的な＿＿＿＿＿を抱く時期。

Aly：17 歳。人にはそれぞれ＿＿＿＿＿＿＿＿＿＿があり、それは変わることなく維持されるものであると考えている。ただ、＿＿＿＿＿には、どんなに揺るぎない自尊心を持っていたとしても＿＿＿＿＿＿＿＿＿＿ことがある、ということは認めている。

The Study

2

1-40

The drop in self-esteem in adolescence was no surprise to Richard Robins, a psychology professor at the University of California at Davis, who spearheaded the study, but ❺ "the drop in old age is a little bit more novel," he said. Specifically, ❻ Robins was intrigued by the **similarities** in self-esteem levels between those entering adolescence and old age. "There is an accumulation of losses occurring all at once both in old age and adolescence," he suggested. "There is a critical mass of **transition** going on."

3

1-41

Those answering the survey ranged in age from 9 to 90. They participated in the survey by logging onto a Web site during a period between 1999 and 2000. About three-quarters were Caucasian, the rest a mixture of people of Asian, black, Latino and Middle-Eastern descent. Most were from the United States. The survey simply asked people to agree or strongly disagree—on a five-point scale—with the statement: "I see myself as someone who has high self-esteem."

4

1-42

Everybody is an individual, Robins stressed, so self-esteem can be affected by a number of things that are biological, social, and situational, but there are certain passages that all of us face—and each passage can have a powerful effect on our sense of self. "With kids, their feelings about themselves are often based on relatively superficial information," Robins explained. "As we get older, we base our self-esteem on actual achievements and **feedback** from other people."

5

1-43

❾ **Overall**, the study indicated that (＿＿＿＿＿＿＿) do not fare as well as (＿＿＿＿＿＿＿) in self-esteem—a difference particularly marked in adolescence. "During adolescence, girls' self-esteem dropped about twice as much as boys'," Robins said, perhaps at least partially because of society's heavy emphasis on body image for girls. Add one negative life event to all of this turmoil, and a teenager's delicate self-esteem can crumble.

NOTES spearhead「…の先頭に立つ」 accumulation「蓄積」 Caucasian「白人の」 descent「家系」
situational「状況による」 superficial「表面的な」 fare「やっていく」 turmoil「混乱」 crumble「崩れる」

❹ このブロック全体（❷〜❺）の内容と一致するものを１つ選びましょう。

    a. A person's self-esteem does not change during adolescence.
    b. The people in the study were mostly Asian.
    c. Our self-esteem is affected by several factors.
    d. Our self-esteem is most delicate when we are adults.

❺ "the drop in old age is a little bit more novel" とは、どのような意味でしょうか。最も適切なものを選びましょう。

    a. The drop in self-esteem in old age is more like a book
    b. The drop in self-esteem in old age is more unusual
    c. The drop in self-esteem in old age is more expected

❻ Robins 氏が興味をそそられたことは何ですか。それを示す箇所に波下線（ ～～ ）を引き、その内容を日本語で答えましょう。

    内容：＿＿＿＿＿＿＿＿＿＿＿＿＿＿＿＿＿＿＿＿＿＿＿＿＿＿＿＿＿＿＿＿＿＿＿

❼ Robins 氏の行った調査の内容について整理しましょう。

    対象年齢：＿＿＿歳から＿＿＿歳まで。

    人種：4分の3は＿＿＿＿＿。その他、＿＿＿＿＿＿＿＿＿＿＿＿＿＿＿＿＿など様々。

    出身：ほとんどが＿＿＿＿＿＿＿＿＿＿＿＿＿＿＿＿。

    調査方法：「＿＿＿＿＿＿＿＿＿＿＿＿＿＿＿＿＿＿＿＿＿＿＿＿＿＿＿＿＿＿＿」という文に対して「そう思う」か「まったくそう思わない」か、＿＿＿＿＿＿＿＿＿で答える。

❽ 成長するにつれて、自尊心の基準は子どものときと比べてどのように変わりますか。

    子どものときは、自己に対する強い感情は、比較的＿＿＿＿＿＿＿＿＿＿に基づく。年齢を重ねるにつれて、自尊心は＿＿＿＿＿＿＿＿＿＿や＿＿＿＿＿＿＿＿＿＿に基づくものとなる。

❾ 第5パラグラフの内容に合うように、"Overall ..." で始まる文の空欄に適する語句をそれぞれ下から選んで入れましょう。

    [younger people / older people / men / women]

Emerging into Adulthood

6

Eileen remembered having fairly high self-esteem from ages 12 to 16. She had been very ill as a child, so the teen years were a time for her to blossom. Then, her mother died when she was 17, and her self-esteem bottomed out. "I was like, 'What do I do? How do I handle this?'" Eileen remembered. Eileen was 22 when she married Fred, an event that **coincided** with the beginning of her adult years—and an upswing in her self-esteem. Like many adults, Eileen gained her senses of competence and **continuity**, both of which can contribute to the rise in self-esteem during the adult years, Robins said.

7

Even if there is divorce or some other form of **chaos**, there has been a change in our ability to cope, he said. We learn with experience. Fred is aware that his sense of self-esteem may be **vulnerable** when he retires. "I'm concerned about keeping my awareness level," he said. "Am I going to be aware of the social scene? Of things more global? Am I going to be able to read and keep up with everything?"

8

Seniors do tend to experience a drop in self-esteem when they get into their 70s, the study says—but not always. This is enigmatic to Robins. "When we look at things like general well-being, the evidence is mixed about what happens in old age," he said.

9

Some people experience a tremendous loss of self-esteem, whereas others maintain their sense of well-being right through old age. Others are not as lucky. ⑮ <u>Whereas adolescents lose their sense of childhood omnipotence, seniors experience another kind of loss.</u> Retirement comes at about the same time seniors may begin to lose loved ones, their health, their financial status, or their sense of competence. Suddenly, someone who was so in charge may become withdrawn, sullen, and depressed. Their self-esteem may plummet. Robins hopes the study will make us more aware of the times when our self-esteem can be in jeopardy.

NOTES blossom「開花する」 bottom out「底に達する」 upswing「上向き」 enigmatic「不思議な」 well-being「幸福」
omnipotence「無限の力」 sullen「不機嫌な」 plummet「急落する」 jeopardy「危険」

⑩ Eileenのこれまでの人生で彼女の自尊心に大きな影響を与えた出来事は何だったでしょう。また、どのような影響を与えましたか。

■17歳：＿＿＿＿＿＿＿＿＿＿＿＿＿＿＿＿＿＿＿

影響：＿＿＿＿＿＿＿＿＿＿＿＿＿＿＿＿＿＿＿

■22歳：＿＿＿＿＿＿＿＿＿＿＿＿＿＿＿＿＿＿＿

影響：＿＿＿＿＿＿＿＿＿＿＿＿＿＿＿＿＿＿＿

❶❶ Robins氏によると、成人期にEileenの自尊心を高めた要因は何ですか。それを示している部分を抜き出しましょう。また、一般的に成人期に自尊心がそれほど落ち込まないのはなぜだと言っていますか。日本語で説明しましょう。

語句：_____

説明：_____

❶❷ 定年を間近に控えたFredは、どのようなことに気をつけていますか。

_____
_____
_____

❶❸ "Whereas ..." で始まる文と同様の内容を表す英文を1つ選びましょう。

　a. Both adolescents and seniors experience the same sense of loss.
　b. Adolescents experience a sense of loss, but seniors do not.
　c. Adolescents and seniors experience a different sense of loss.

❶❹ 第8、9パラグラフの内容をまとめましょう。

研究では、高齢者は70代に入ったとき自尊心の落ち込みを経験する傾向にあるという結果が出ているが、_____。自尊心を喪失してしまう人もいれば、幸福感を維持する人もいる。高齢者が直面する喪失は様々で、_____、_____、_____、自分の能力などである。それらが、_____と同じ時期に訪れる。

❶❺ Robins氏はこの研究をどのように役立てたいと思っていますか。

_____
_____

UNIT 2　HEALTH AND WELL-BEING

Information Organization

▶ 下の図と表を使って、本文の内容を整理しましょう。空欄にあてはまる語を英語で記入しましょう。空欄に入る語は1語とは限りません。

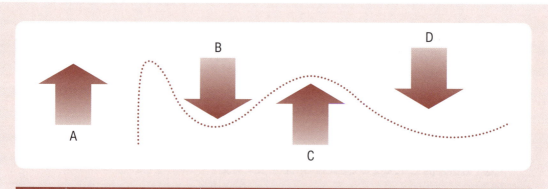

Stage	Age	Reasons for the Self-esteem Change
A	(1.)	Feeling about themselves are often based on relatively (2.); high childhood (3.): inflated sense of self-approval
B	(4.)	Loss of (5.); society's emphasis on body image for (6.)
C	(7.)	Gain a sense of competence and (8.); development of ability to (9.) with change
D	Senior	(10.); loss of loved ones, (11.), (12.), or sense of competence

Short Summary

▶ 空欄に適する単語を記入して、本文全体の要約文を完成させましょう。

Throughout a person's lifetime, it is most likely that his or her self-esteem will follow a course similar to a (1.   ), filled with ups and downs. Beginning with (2.   ), people experience an inflated sense of self-approval based on relatively superficial information. With changes in hormones and an increased sense of self-doubt, adolescents experience a plunge in their level of self-esteem. As people grow into (3.   ), they tend to gain a sense of competence and continuity, along with the ability to deal with change, which enables self-esteem to (4.   ). In their 70s, seniors tend to experience a (5.   ) in self-esteem due to retirement, a decrease in capabilities, or the loss of loved ones.

Critical Thinking

▶ 以下の質問について自分の意見をまとめましょう。そして、ペアやグループで話し合ったり、クラスで発表したりしましょう。

1. The author states that "There is an accumulation of losses occurring all at once, both in old age and adolescence." What losses do you think occur at these two stages of our lives? Why do you think so?

2. What are some ways that adolescents can maintain their sense of self-esteem in spite of the losses they experience? What advice would you give an adolescent who is suffering a drop in self-esteem?

CHAPTER 5

Who Lives Longer?

Pre-reading Preparation

▶ 誰もが健康で長生きをしたいと考えます。長生きと関係があると思われるものを次の中から選んでチェックしましょう（複数回答可）。

- ☐ education
- ☐ environment
- ☐ exercise
- ☐ health care
- ☐ income
- ☐ meal
- ☐ sleep
- ☐ stress

Vocabulary

▶ 下の語句の意味を調べ、表に記入しましょう。次に、英語の説明として適切なものを枠内から選び、記号で答えましょう。

語句	意味	説明
1. longevity		
2. landmark		
3. profound		
4. beneficial		
5. autonomy		

語句	意味	説明
6. satisfaction		
7. immune		
8. suppress		
9. hypothesis		
10. acquaintance		

a. someone you know, but who is not a close friend
b. the ability to make your own decisions without being influenced by anyone else
c. producing results that bring advantages
d. an idea that may explain what is not yet tested or proven
e. having strength biologically to fight against infection of one's body
f. an event, change, or discovery that influences someone or something
g. the length of a person or animal's life
h. important and having strong influence or effect
i. happiness or pleasure because you have achieved or gotten something
j. to prevent something from growing or developing, or from working effectively

Reading Analysis

▶ 英文を読んで、問いに答えましょう。

1

How to live longer is a topic that has fascinated mankind for centuries. Today, scientists are beginning to separate the facts from the fallacies surrounding the aging process. Why is it that some people reach a ripe old age and others do not? Several factors influencing **longevity** are set at birth, but surprisingly, many others are elements that can be changed. Here is ❶ what you should know.

2

Some researchers divide the elements determining who will live longer into two categories: fixed factors and changeable factors. Gender, race and heredity are fixed factors—they cannot be reversed, although certain long-term social changes can influence them. For example, women live longer than men—at birth, their life expectancy is about seven to eight years more. However, cigarette smoking, drinking and reckless driving could shorten this advantage.

3

There is increasing evidence that length of life is also influenced by a number of elements that are within your ability to control. The most obvious are ❸ physical lifestyle factors.

NOTES fallacy「誤った考え」 heredity「遺伝」 expectancy「予測値、期待値」

❶ 「私たちが知っておくべきもの」とは、どのようなことでしょうか。

人の寿命に＿＿＿＿＿＿ものには、＿＿＿＿＿＿のものもあるが、＿＿＿＿＿＿＿＿＿＿＿＿ものも多いということ。私たちはこれを知っておくべきである。

❷ 寿命を延ばす要因として考えられるものをまとめましょう。

- 不変的な要因：性別、＿＿＿＿、＿＿＿＿
- 可変的な要因：＿＿＿＿、飲酒、＿＿＿＿＿

❸ "physical lifestyle factors" とは、どのような要因でしょうか。

寿命の長さに影響を与える要因のうち、＿＿＿＿＿＿＿＿＿＿＿＿＿＿＿＿＿＿＿＿。

UNIT 2 HEALTH AND WELL-BEING

[_____] Measures

4
1-51

According to a **landmark** study of nearly 7,000 adults in Alameda County, California, women can add up to seven years to their lives and men 11 to 12 years by following seven simple health practices: (1) Do not smoke. (2) If you drink, do so only moderately. (3) Eat breakfast regularly. (4) Do not eat between meals. (5) Maintain normal weight. (6) Sleep about eight hours a night. (7) Exercise moderately.

5
1-52

Cutting calories may be the single most significant lifestyle change you can make. Experiments have shown that in laboratory animals, a 40 percent calorie reduction leads to a 50 percent extension in longevity. "Eating less has a more **profound** and diversified effect on the aging process than does any other lifestyle change," says Byung P. Yu, Ph.D., professor of physiology at the University of Texas Health Science Center at San Antonio. "It is the only factor we know of in laboratory animals that is an anti-aging factor."

NOTES moderately「適度に」

❹ ここで挙げられている 7 つの項目を実行すると、どのような効果が現れると筆者は述べていますか。また、その 7 項目は全体としてどのようなことでしょうか。

効果：_____が延びる。

7 項目：変えると良い 7 つの_____。

❺ 第 5 パラグラフで述べられている実験についてまとめましょう。

動物実験の結果：_____

結論：_____

❻ このブロック（**4** と **5**）はどのようなことを述べているでしょうか。また、本文中の見出しの空欄に適語を記入しましょう。

老化防止対策のうち、_____に関するものを述べている。

Psychosocial Factors

6 1-53

A long life, ❼ (   ), is not just the result of being good to your body and staving off disease. All the various factors that constitute and influence daily life can be critical too. In searching for the ingredients to a long, healthy existence, scientists are studying links between longevity and the psychological and social aspects of human existence. The following can play significant roles in determining your longevity:

❼ 本文中の空欄に適語を記入しましょう。また、その語句が入る理由を考えましょう。

理由：前のブロック（**4**と**5**）で長生きの要因として＿＿＿＿＿＿について述べているが、空欄のあとに＿＿＿＿＿＿という語句が出てきて、＿＿＿＿＿＿＿＿＿＿＿＿＿＿ことだけが長生きの要因ではないと述べ、さらに次の文で最後にtooが出てきて、＿＿＿＿＿＿に関する情報が＿＿＿＿されているから。

Social Integration

7 1-54

Researchers have found that people who are socially integrated—they are part of a family network, are married, participate in structured group activities—live longer.

8 1-55

Early studies indicated that the more friends and relatives you had, the longer you lived. Newer studies focus on the types of relationships that are most **beneficial**. "Larger networks don't always seem to be advantageous to women," says epidemiologist Teresa Seeman, Ph.D., associate research scientist at Yale University. "Certain kinds of ties add more demands rather than generate more help."

NOTES epidemiologist「疫（病）学者」

❽ 小見出しの *Social Integration* には、どのような日本語訳が適切でしょうか。また、そう考える理由は何でしょうか。

Social Integration：＿＿＿＿＿＿＿＿＿＿＿＿＿＿

理由：研究者は、社会の中でうまく＿＿＿＿＿＿＿を築いた人がより＿＿＿＿＿＿と考えているが、初期の研究が単に結びつきの＿＿＿＿＿を寿命の長さの要因と捉えていたのに対して、最近では結びついている＿＿＿＿＿＿＿＿＿＿によって違うと考えられていることを説明しているから。

Autonomy

❾ A feeling of **autonomy** or control can come from having a say in important decisions (where you live, how you spend your money) or from being surrounded by people who inspire confidence in your ability to master certain tasks (yes, you can quit smoking, you will get well). Studies show these feelings bring a sense of well-being and **satisfaction** with life. "Autonomy is a key factor in successful aging," says Toni Antonucci, associate research scientist at the Institute for Social Research at the University of Michigan.

❾ 下線部内の "having a say" の言い換えとして最も適切なものを選びましょう。また、それを参考にして下線部を訳しましょう。

言い換え： a. having an opinion
　　　　　 b. having a choice
　　　　　 c. speaking loudly

訳：＿＿＿＿＿＿＿＿＿＿＿＿＿＿＿＿＿＿＿＿＿＿＿＿＿＿＿＿＿＿＿＿＿＿＿＿＿

Stress and Job Satisfaction

Researchers disagree on how these factors affect longevity. There is not enough data available to support a link between stress and longevity, says Edward L. Schneider, M.D., dean of the Andrus Gerontology Center at the University of Southern California. Animal research, however, provides exciting insights. In studies with laboratory rats, certain types of stress damage the **immune** system and destroy brain cells, especially those involved in memory. Other kinds of stress enhance immune function by 20 to 30 percent, supporting a theory first advanced by Hans Selye, M.D., Ph.D., a pioneer in stress research. He proposed that an exciting, active and meaningful life contributes to good health.

The relationship between job satisfaction and longevity also remains in question. According to some researchers, a satisfying job adds years to a man's life, while volunteer work increases a woman's longevity. These findings may change as more women participate in the workforce. One study found that clerical workers suffered twice as many heart attacks as homemakers. Factors associated with the coronary problems were **suppressed** hostility, having a nonsupportive boss, and decreased job mobility.

NOTES gerontology「老年学」(老人や老人問題などの研究)　immune system「免疫システム」
clerical「事務の」　coronary「心臓の」

 ストレスや仕事に対する満足感が寿命に及ぼす影響について、どのように述べられているかをまとめましょう。

- **ストレス**：影響は＿＿＿＿が、研究者によって意見が＿＿＿＿＿。まだ寿命をストレスと結びつける＿＿＿＿は少ないが、＿＿＿＿＿によると、ストレスは＿＿＿＿＿を低下させたり、＿＿＿＿＿することがわかっている。

- **仕事に対する満足感**：影響について、まだわからない部分が＿＿＿＿＿。男性は、仕事に対する＿＿＿＿＿＿と寿命が延びる。これに対して、女性は＿＿＿＿＿＿＿＿のほうが寿命を延ばす。たとえば＿＿＿＿＿と関連のある因子には、抑え込んだ反感、＿＿＿＿＿＿上司、転職の機会の減少などがあって、＿＿＿＿＿に就いている人のほうが、専業主婦よりも心臓発作を＿＿＿＿＿＿＿＿＿＿は２倍にもなるのである。

Environment

12 Where you live can make a difference in how long you live. A study by the California Department of Health Services in Berkeley found a 40 percent higher mortality rate among people living in a poverty area compared to those in a nonpoverty area. "The difference was not due to age, sex, health care or lifestyle," says George A. Kaplan, Ph.D., chief of the department's Human Population Laboratory. The resulting **hypothesis**: ⓫ <u>A locale can have environmental characteristics, such as polluted air or water, or socioeconomic characteristics, such as a high crime rate and level of stress, that make it unhealthy.</u>

NOTES Berkeley「米国カリフォルニア州バークリー市」 socioeconomic「社会経済的な」

⓫ このパラグラフのトピックセンテンスに波下線（ ～～ ）を引きましょう。また、"A locale ..."で始まる文は何を示しているか考えましょう。

このパラグラフでは寿命の長さは＿＿＿＿＿＿＿＿＿＿によって異なるということを述べているが、この文は健康に＿＿＿＿＿影響をもたらす＿＿＿＿地域の特性（＿＿＿＿特徴と＿＿＿＿＿＿特徴）およびその具体例を示している。

Socioeconomic Status

13 People with higher incomes, more education and high-status occupations tend to live longer. Researchers used to think this was due to better living and job conditions, ⓬ <u>nutrition and access to health care</u>, but these theories have not held up. Nevertheless, the differences can be dramatic. Among women 65 to 74 years old, those with less than an eighth-grade education are much more likely to die than are women who have completed at least one year of college.

⓬ "nutrition and access to health care"とは、どのようなことを表しているか説明しましょう。

＿＿＿＿＿＿＿＿＿＿＿＿＿＿＿＿＿＿＿＿＿＿＿＿＿＿＿＿＿＿＿＿＿＿＿＿＿＿
＿＿＿＿＿＿＿＿＿＿＿＿＿＿＿＿＿＿＿＿＿＿＿＿＿＿＿＿＿＿＿＿＿＿＿＿＿＿

⓭ 小見出しの"Socioeconomic"とは、どのようなことを表す語でしょうか。前のパラグラフの内容も踏まえ、[ ]内の語句を使って推測してみましょう。

[経済活動、社会活動、収入、教育]

「社会経済的」と訳されるが、＿＿＿＿＿＿＿＿＿＿＿＿＿＿＿＿＿＿＿＿＿＿＿＿
＿＿＿＿＿＿＿＿＿＿＿＿＿＿＿＿＿＿＿＿＿＿＿＿＿＿＿＿＿＿＿＿＿＿＿＿＿＿
＿＿＿＿＿＿＿＿＿＿＿＿＿＿＿＿＿＿＿＿＿＿＿＿＿＿＿＿＿＿＿＿＿＿＿＿＿＿

What Can You Do?

The message from the experts is clear. There are many ways to add years to your life. Instituting sound health practices and expanding your circle of **acquaintances** and activities will have a beneficial effect. The good news about aging, observes Erdman B. Palmore of the Center for the Study of Aging and Human Development at Duke Medical Center in North Carolina, is many of the factors related to longevity are also related to life satisfaction.

NOTES sound「健全な」

⓮ 専門家が寿命について述べていることをまとめましょう。

寿命を＿＿＿＿＿方法は＿＿＿＿＿＿ある。健全な＿＿＿＿＿＿を作ることと＿＿＿＿＿＿＿＿を広げることは、＿＿＿＿＿＿＿＿＿方法である。寿命を延ばす要因には、＿＿＿＿＿＿＿＿＿＿＿＿＿＿＿＿と関係のあるものが＿＿＿＿＿。

⓯ 筆者は寿命を延ばす方法について、特にどの点に共感しているかを、そう判断した理由とともにまとめましょう。

_____
_____
_____

Information Organization

▶ 下の表を使って、本文の内容を整理しましょう。空欄にあてはまる語を英語で記入しましょう。空欄に入る語は１語とは限りません。

Who Lives Longer?		
(1.)	**Changeable factors**	
1. gender 2. (2.) 3. (3.)	**Health** (4.) 1. don't smoke 2. drink moderately 3. eat (5.) 4. don't (6.) between meals 5. maintain normal weight 6. sleep (7.) 7. (8.)	(9.) **factors** 1. (10.) integration 2. (11.) 3. stress and job (12.) 4. environment 5. (13.) status
What you can do: 1. Institute sound (14.) 2. Expand your circle of (15.)		

Short Summary

▶ 空欄に適する単語を記入して、本文全体の要約文を完成させましょう。

Our longevity is affected by many (1.   ). Some of them, such as gender, race, and heredity, are (2.   ). However, others are (3.   ). We can take measures to improve our health—for example, get exercise and sleep eight hours every night. (4.   ) factors, such as our level of autonomy, the amount of stress in our lives, and the number of friends we have, also affect our (5.   ) and are under our control.

Critical Thinking

▶ 以下の質問について自分の意見をまとめましょう。そして、ペアやグループで話し合ったり、クラスで発表したりしましょう。

1. Why do you think volunteer work increases a woman's longevity?

2. What are some of the consequences of an aging population? In other words, what factors must be taken into consideration as the elderly begin to make up a larger segment of a country's population than ever before? What needs will have to be met?

CHAPTER 6

Are Gifted Children Born or Made?

Pre-reading Preparation

▶ 若い頃から才能を開花させた天才として知られるのは誰でしょうか。次の中から選んでチェックしましょう（複数回答可）。

☐ Albert Einstein　　☐ Alfred Nobel　　☐ Ichiro　　☐ Madam Curie
☐ Michael Jackson　　☐ Pablo Picasso　　☐ Steve Jobs　　☐ Wolfgang Amadeus Mozart

Vocabulary

▶ 下の語句の意味を調べ、表に記入しましょう。次に、英語の説明として適切なものを枠内から選び、記号で答えましょう。

語句	意味	説明	語句	意味	説明
1. expertise			6. undermine		
2. quit			7. prestigious		
3. obsession			8. invest		
4. rage			9. due to		
5. contemporary			10. compose		

a. to stop doing something
b. to weaken the effectiveness, power, or ability of something
c. special skill or knowledge that is acquired by training, study, or practice
d. to spend a lot of time or energy on something that you consider to be useful
e. to write or create a piece of music
f. a strong desire or passion
g. a person who is or was alive at the same time as another
h. being respected and admired by people
i. caused by something; as a direct result of something
j. an idea or thought that continually preoccupies a person's mind

CHAPTER 6　Are Gifted Children Born or Made?

Reading Analysis

▶ 英文を読んで、問いに答えましょう。

1　Some say given enough time, money and instruction, any child can develop a special **expertise**. Others, ❷ (　　　　　　　　), insist gifted children are born, not made.

❶ 天才児に関して二分する意見とは、どのようなものでしょうか。

十分な時間、資金、指導があれば、＿＿＿＿＿＿＿＿＿＿＿＿＿＿

ができると考える人と、天才児は＿＿＿＿＿＿であって、＿＿＿＿＿＿＿＿

と主張する人がいる。

❷ 本文中の空欄に最も適切な語句を下から選び、記入しましょう。

[therefore / for example / however / also]

A Rage to Master

2　Gaven Largent, 13, has been playing music for five years. He started with guitar lessons at age eight, but not long after, he **quit**—not making music, just taking lessons. "I was not learning anything," he says. "I was just playing those notes on the paper; it was boring."

3　"Gaven became frustrated that it was sheet music and he was only playing the notes on the music," his mother Melissa says. "He wanted to fill it in and make it more." She says they knew when he was nine or ten that music would be his focus. "It became an **obsession** for him to figure out the sounds that he heard on a CD or the radio or live music."

4　That obsession is one of the trademarks of a gifted child, or prodigy, according to developmental psychologist Ellen Winner, who teaches at Boston College. "I say they have a **rage** to master. It is difficult to tear them away from the area in which they have high ability."

NOTES　note「音符」　sheet music「楽譜」　prodigy「天才」　developmental psychologist「発達心理学者」

❸ なぜGaven Largentはギターのレッスンを辞めたのでしょうか。

Because he felt that he was not learning (　　　　　　　　) and he became (　　　　　　).

UNIT 2   HEALTH AND WELL-BEING

❹ Gaven Largent の音楽の才能を示すエピソードに波下線（ ～～～ ）を引き、その内容を日本語で答えましょう。

内容：＿＿＿＿＿＿＿＿＿＿＿＿＿＿＿＿＿＿＿＿＿＿＿＿＿＿＿＿＿＿＿＿＿＿

❺ Ellen Winner の天才児に関する見解について、まとめましょう。

＿＿＿＿＿＿＿＿＿＿＿＿＿＿＿＿が天才児の特徴の1つで、天才児は何かを究めようと切望し、＿＿＿＿＿

＿＿＿＿＿＿＿＿＿＿＿＿＿＿＿＿＿＿＿＿から彼らを引き離すのは困難である。

❻ 見出し A Rage to Master を言い換えられる語句を第2〜4パラグラフの中から抜き出しましょう。

＿＿＿＿＿＿＿＿＿＿＿＿＿＿＿＿

Looking Back as Former Child Prodigies

5
1-66

Julian Lage, who is now 21, remembers playing guitar for hours as a child. ❼"You wake up and you eat and you play music and you sleep." Lage, who recently released his first CD, *Sounding Point*, started playing guitar at five. A few years later, he was the subject of a documentary film, *Jules at Eight*. Still, the title "child prodigy" was something he never felt he could relate to. ❾"Younger musicians, my **contemporaries** who have been called child prodigies, they feel slighted because it does **undermine** the work ethic, the thousands of hours you put in just to be able to produce a sound on your instrument."

6
1-67

❿ That is a sentiment echoed by Rasta Thomas, 27, who was also labeled a prodigy. He made dance history as a teenager, winning the Gold Medal in the Senior Men's Division of the **prestigious** Jackson International Ballet Competition in Jackson, Mississippi at the age of 14. He now headlines his own dance company, Bad Boys of Dance. "I think if you give any seven-year-old the training I had, you will get a product that is ⓫ at the top of its game," Thomas says. "I have had hours and hours and a million dollars **invested** into the training that I received."

NOTES   slighted「軽んじられて」 work ethic「労働意識、労働倫理」
the Jackson International Ballet Competition「ジャクソン国際バレエコンクール：4年に1度開催され、格式が高い」
headline「…の主役を務める」

❼ "You wake up and you eat and you play music and you sleep." は何を意味しているでしょうか。

   a. Julian Lage never went to school.
   b. Julian Lage did not sleep a lot.
   c. Julian Lage played music all day.

❽ Julian Lage と Rasta Thomas について、次の表にまとめましょう。

	年齢	最近の業績	天才児と呼ばれる理由
Lage	21		5歳で＿＿＿＿＿＿＿＿、数年後、天才児として＿＿＿＿＿＿＿＿＿
Thomas	27		幼いころからダンスを始め、14歳のとき、名高いバレエコンクールで＿＿＿＿＿＿

❾ "Younger musicians," で始まる文を訳しましょう。

＿＿＿＿＿＿＿＿＿＿＿＿＿＿＿＿＿＿＿＿＿＿＿＿＿＿＿＿＿＿

＿＿＿＿＿＿＿＿＿＿＿＿＿＿＿＿＿＿＿＿＿＿＿＿＿＿＿＿＿＿

＿＿＿＿＿＿＿＿＿＿＿＿＿＿＿＿＿＿＿＿＿＿＿＿＿＿＿＿＿＿

❿ "That is a sentiment echoed by Rasta Thomas" と同様の内容を表す英文を1つ選びましょう。

　a. Rasta Thomas felt sorry for Julia Lage.
　b. Rasta Thomas had a similar feeling about being called a child prodigy.
　c. Rasta Thomas felt sentimental about being called a child prodigy.

⓫ "at the top of its game" は何を意味しているでしょうか。最も適切なものを選びましょう。

　a. the highest level
　b. the winner of the game
　c. the best player of the game

⓬ 天才児と呼ばれることについて、Thomasはどのように考えているでしょうか。

自分と同じだけの時間や費用を投資すれば、＿＿＿＿＿＿＿＿＿＿＿＿＿＿＿。つまり、自分が成功したのは＿＿＿＿＿＿＿ではなく、＿＿＿＿＿＿からなのだ。

Enabling Talent to Flower

7

But Winner, the author of *Gifted Children: Myths and Realities*, disagrees. "You can't make a gifted child out of any child." Winner says prodigies are born with natural talent, but she does believe they "need to be enabled in order to have their ability flower." Both Julian Lage, who played with vibraphonist, Gary Burton at age 12, and Rasta Thomas, who studied at the Kirov Ballet Academy in Washington, say they had that support. But the success that both Lage and Thomas enjoy today as adults is **due to** much more. Winner says studies have shown that ⑭ most music prodigies are unheard of as adults. "The gift of being a child prodigy is very different from the gift of being an adult creator," she says. "To be an adult creator means you have to do something new, which means ⑮ taking a risk." Both Lage and Thomas took that creative risk early, **composing** and choreographing while they were still in their teens. Gaven Largent is headed in that direction as well. "I do write," he says. "I have not written too many songs with lyrics, but that's something I'd like to work on." Right now, he adds, he is working on a gospel song.

NOTES enable ... to *do*「…が〜できるようにする」 vibraphonist「ビブラフォン奏者」
the Kirov Ballet Academy「キーロフ・バレエ・アカデミー：1989年創立の世界的に有名なバレエ学校」
choreograph「振付をする」 lyrics「歌詞」

⓭ 第7パラグラフの中で、天才児に関するWinner氏の考えを最もよく表す文に波下線を引き、その内容を日本語で答えましょう。

内容：＿＿＿＿＿＿＿＿＿＿＿＿＿＿＿＿＿＿＿＿＿＿＿＿＿＿＿＿＿＿＿＿

⓮ "most music prodigies are unheard of as adults."と同様の内容になるように、空欄に適語を入れましょう。

most music prodigies do not become (　　　　　　　) when they are adults

⓯ Lage, Thomas, Largentそれぞれの"taking a risk"の具体例を答えましょう。

Lage：＿＿＿＿＿＿＿＿＿＿

Thomas：＿＿＿＿＿＿＿＿＿＿

Largent：＿＿＿＿＿＿＿＿＿＿＿＿＿＿

Information Organization

▶ 下の表を使って、本文の内容を整理しましょう。空欄1〜13にあてはまる語を英語で記入しましょう。空欄に入る語は1語とは限りません。また、空欄a〜cには本文から名前を抜き出して記入しましょう。

Name of psychologist	Ellen Winner
What is her profession?	She is a (1.) who teaches at Boston College. She is also the author of the book, *Gifted Children: Myths and Realities*.
Does she believe gifted children are born or made?	She does not think you can make a (2.) child out of any child. She believes prodigies are born with a (3.), but need to be enabled in order to have their ability (4.).

Name of prodigy	How does this person excel?	How does this person feel about being called a child prodigy? Why?
(a.)	He only took guitar lessons for a short time, but was able to (5.) the sounds that he heard on a CD or the (6.) or live music. Now he (7.) his own music.	
(b.)	He is a musical (8.) who started playing guitar at age 5. He was the subject of a (9.) film.	He does not like the title "child prodigy" because it (10.) the thousands of hours that he spent practicing.
(c.)	He is a child prodigy in (11.), and won the Gold Medal at the Jackson International Ballet Competition when he was 14. He now has his own (12.).	He does not like the title "child prodigy" either, because he believes that his success is a result of his (13.).

UNIT 2　HEALTH AND WELL-BEING

Short Summary

▶ 空欄に適する単語を記入して、本文全体の要約文を完成させましょう。

While some people state that child (1.   ) can be made, it appears that child prodigies are born with an innate (2.   ) in a particular area, such as (3.   ) or dance. Furthermore, children reveal this special ability at an early age. However, the talent must be (4.   ), or nurtured, in order for it to (5.   ).

Critical Thinking

▶ 以下の質問について自分の意見をまとめましょう。そして、ペアやグループで話し合ったり、クラスで発表したりしましょう。

1. Some child prodigies who are extremely young go to universities. Do you think this is a good environment for these children? Why or why not? Explain your answer, and give examples to support your opinion.

2. Imagine you discover that your young son or daughter is a child prodigy. What will you do? How will you encourage your child? How will you protect your son's or daughter's childhood?

UNIT 3

THE ENVIRONMENT

CHAPTER 7

Students Dig into Sustainable Farming at Vermont College

Pre-reading Preparation

▶ 今までに家庭菜園や農業に携わった経験はありますか。育てたことのある動物や植物にチェックを入れましょう（複数回答可）。

☐ chicken　　☐ cow　　☐ horse　　☐ pig　　☐ sheep
☐ cucumber　☐ eggplant　☐ rice　　☐ rose　☐ tulip

Vocabulary

▶ 下の語句の意味を調べ、表に記入しましょう。次に、英語の説明として適切なものを枠内から選び、記号で答えましょう。

語句	意味	説明	語句	意味	説明
1. plow			6. regional		
2. intensive			7. application		
3. sustainable			8. enlightened		
4. agriculture			9. draft		
5. organic			10. suburban		

a. the practice or science of farming
b. the purpose for which a machine, idea, etc. can be used, or the act of using it
c. used for pulling heavy loads
d. showing understanding of something, and not believing it false
e. involving a lot of activity, effort, or careful attention in a short period of time
f. grown or raised without using artificial chemicals
g. to cut the earth
h. relating to a particular area of a country or of the world
i. relating to an area away from the downtown, where a lot of people live
j. continuing or lasting for a long time

Reading Analysis

▶ 英文を読んで、問いに答えましょう。

1

Devin Lyons typically starts his days this summer cooking breakfast with fresh eggs from the farm's ❶ chicken coop. Then, depending on the weather, he and a dozen other college students might cut hay in the field using a team of oxen, turn compost, or weed vegetable beds.

1
2
3
4

NOTES　compost「堆肥」　weed vegetable bed「野菜の畝（うね）の雑草を抜く」

❶ "chicken coop"とは、どのようなものでしょうか。下から1つ選びましょう。

a. a refrigerator for chicken eggs
b. a small building for chickens
c. a food store on a farm

❷ このパラグラフの役割を考え、読み取れることを確認しましょう。

話の_____。"typically"や"this summer"といった語句から、この夏_____で_____行われることが示されているのがわかり、またその後の記述（例えば"other student"）などから、これは農業を学ぶ_____の話であり、学生たちは夏の_____を行っているのだと読み取れる。

67

UNIT 3　THE ENVIRONMENT

While other college students are in stuffy classrooms, about a dozen are earning credit tending a Vermont farm. For 13 weeks, 12 credits and about $12,500, the Green Mountain College students **plow** fields with oxen or horses, milk cows, weed crops, and grow and make their own food, part of an **intensive** course in **sustainable agriculture** using the least amount of fossil fuels. "Lots of schools study sustainable agriculture, but I don't think any of them put it into practice," said spokesman Kevin Coburn.

NOTES　stuffy「息が詰まるような」　put ... into practice「…を実際に行う」

❸ 次の質問の答えとして適切なほうを選び、その理由を日本語で述べましょう。

According to the author, which is preferable for college students studying farming?
- a. Sitting in a stuffy classroom
- b. Being outside doing farm work

理由：＿＿＿＿＿＿＿＿＿＿＿＿＿＿＿＿＿＿＿＿＿＿＿＿＿＿＿＿＿＿＿＿＿＿＿

❹ "sustainable agriculture"は「持続可能型農業」と呼ばれますが、どのようなところがこの農業の特徴を表していると思いますか。推測してみましょう。

There are no tractors on the 22 acres next to the brick campus of the small liberal arts college on the edge of the town—just two teams of oxen, and goats, pigs, two cows, and chickens. Students sleep in tents on the field's edge, next to a river. They spend about six hours a week in classes in the old farmhouse, learning theory on **organic** crop and animal management, management of farm systems, development of agricultural technologies with a focus on human and animal power, and the social and cultural importance of **regional** food. The rest of the time they are out in the field, or doing homework and working on research projects. "So they're actually seeing the **applications** ❺ firsthand," said Kenneth Mulder, manager of the college's Cerridwen Farm, who runs the summer program.

❺ "firsthand"は何を表しているでしょうか。下から1つ選びましょう。

- a. By learning about the applications in class
- b. By watching their teachers perform the applications
- c. By doing the applications themselves

❻ 第2パラグラフで「持続可能型農業を実践している」と述べられていますが、このパラグラフではどのような取り組みが行われているのか考えましょう。

＿＿エーカーもの土地では＿＿＿＿＿＿が使用されておらず、＿＿＿＿＿に牛をはじめとする家畜がいる。学生は＿＿＿＿で眠るが、農場内の母屋で＿＿＿を学ぶこともある。その内容には、＿＿＿＿農業や＿＿＿＿＿の力を中心にして農業を進めていく技術などが含まれ、＿＿＿＿にこれを行っていることになる。

4
2-05

College farming is growing. According to the Rodale Institute in Pennsylvania, more than 80 schools now have hands-on and classroom-based farm programs. Many of them are organic vegetable farms, but students do not necessarily earn as many credits as Green Mountain College students do, nor do they get to work with teams of oxen. Sterling College, also in Vermont, has a similar program. ❽ "It's traditionally been one of the leaders in environmental studies and it is because they put their studies where their mouth is in really getting students out and doing and practicing the sort of environmentally **enlightened** work that some talk about in class," said Roland King, a spokesman for the National Association of Independent Colleges and Universities.

❼ 現在、大学における農業はどのようになっているのかまとめましょう。

＿＿＿＿＿の大学で、実践的なものと＿＿＿＿＿＿＿＿をベースにした＿＿＿＿＿＿＿を行っている。その多くは＿＿＿＿＿＿による野菜の生産を行うが、必ずしもグリーンマウンテン大学の学生ほど多くの＿＿＿＿を取得するとは＿＿＿＿＿し、作業で牛を＿＿＿＿＿もない。

❽ "It's traditionally ..." で始まる文を訳して、バーモント州のスターリング大学で同じようなプログラムが行われてきた経緯を理解しましょう。

＿＿＿＿＿＿＿＿＿＿＿＿＿＿＿＿＿＿＿＿＿＿＿＿＿＿＿＿＿＿＿＿＿＿＿＿＿＿
＿＿＿＿＿＿＿＿＿＿＿＿＿＿＿＿＿＿＿＿＿＿＿＿＿＿＿＿＿＿＿＿＿＿＿＿＿＿
＿＿＿＿＿＿＿＿＿＿＿＿＿＿＿＿＿＿＿＿＿＿＿＿＿＿＿＿＿＿＿＿＿＿＿＿＿＿

For her research project, Cassie Callahan, 18, Conway, N.H., wants to water plants with ⁹ <u>gray water</u> collected from the farm's solar shower, attached to the greenhouse. But she is not sure yet if the soap—even biodegradable soap—will harm the plants if it is not diluted. Her real love is working with **draft** horses. She jumps at the chance every time and even has a new tattoo of a team of horses on her shin. In her hometown, she had a job driving horse-drawn sleighs and wagons and now has learned the animals can be used for more than tourism. She hopes to be a farmer, supporting herself and selling a little on the side. "You know, people have jobs to make money to feed themselves and clothe themselves but I'd much rather have my job be to feed and clothe myself," she said.

NOTES solar shower「太陽熱を利用した温水シャワー」 biodegradable「生物分解性の」 shin「むこうずね」
horse-drawn「馬が引く」 support *one*self「自活する」 on the side「副業として」

❾ "gray water"とは、どのような水でしょうか。下から１つ選びましょう。

   a. very dirty
   b. a little dirty
   c. clean, but not clear

❿ Cassie Callahan についてまとめましょう。

年齢	＿＿＿＿歳	出身地	ニューハンプシャー州コンウェイ
希望している農作業			＿＿＿＿付属のシャワー使用後の水で＿＿＿＿をやる。
懸念していること			シャワーの水を＿＿＿＿使ったとしたら、＿＿＿＿の成分が植物に＿＿＿＿ないかどうか。
本当にやりたいこと			＿＿＿作業で＿＿を使いたい。＿＿＿＿ための農業。余ったものを＿＿＿＿売りたい。つまり、自分で食べるものは＿＿＿＿作りたい。

6 🎧 2-07

Green Mountain College hopes to turn out farmers and has several alumni running farms nearby. Other students are interested in food-related fields—whether it is organizing nonprofits, working on policy or overseas development work. Lyons, 19, does not know if he will farm but so far he has learned a lot. Growing up in **suburban** Jefferson, N.J., he said he did not know much about where his food came from and was never exposed to organic farms. "I never really got the connection between the cooked chicken on my plate—and it was a dead chicken that was killed—I just never really thought about it," he said.

NOTES alumni > alumnus「同窓会」 nonprofit「非営利の」

⓫ グリーンマウンテン大学が求めている卒業生像と実情についてまとめましょう。

_____
_____
_____

⓬ 19歳のLyonsは農場を経営するかどうかは決めていないと言いますが、大学に入ってどんなことを学んだと言っているか考えましょう。

都市近郊で育ったため、_____ に触れたこともなく、自分の食べるものが _____ _____ 食卓に上るのかなど意識して _____ 。

⓭ Lyonsは何を表す具体例として、このパラグラフで描かれているのか考えましょう。

_____ ことで、_____ を示すようになった学生の具体例として登場している。

Information Organization

▶ 下の表を使って、本文の内容を整理しましょう。空欄にあてはまる語を英語で記入しましょう。空欄に入る語は1語とは限りません。

Sustainable Farming Program at Green Mountain College	
Location of Program	Green Mountain College, Vermont
Length of Program	13 weeks
(1.) of Program	$12,500
Number of (2.)	12 credits
Types of Classes	Theory on (3.) and animal management, management of farm systems, development of agricultural technologies, and (4.) importance of regional food.
Types of Field Work	Plow field with (5.), milk cows, weed crops, and grow and make their own food using the least amount of (6.).
(7.) of Research Project	Cassie Callahan wants to water plants with gray water collected from the farm's (8.), attached to the green house.
Purpose of Program	Green Mountain College hopes to (9.).
Differences between Green Mountain College and Other Farm Programs	Many schools study (10.), but not all of them put it (11.).

Short Summary

▶ 空欄に適する単語を記入して、本文全体の要約文を完成させましょう。

At some U.S. colleges, students learn about (¹.   ) farming, and get (².   ) experience working with farm animals and growing crops using (³.   ) friendly methods. The students in these programs feel they are learning about where their (⁴.   ) really comes from. It is hoped that many students will set up (⁵.   ) on their own after graduation.

Critical Thinking

▶ 以下の質問について自分の意見をまとめましょう。そして、ペアやグループで話し合ったり、クラスで発表したりしましょう。

1. Organically grown food tends to be more expensive than food grown using chemical fertilizers and insecticides. What are the advantages and disadvantages of growing food organically?

2. Sustainable farming is important to the environment. What are some things you can do every day to help the environment? Make list, and then compare your list with your classmates' lists.

CHAPTER 8

Wilder Places for Wild Things

Pre-reading Preparation

▶ あなたは動物園というと、どのようなことばを連想しますか。連想できる語句を次の中から選んでチェックしましょう（複数回答可）。

- ☐ concrete cage
- ☐ electric monorail
- ☐ jungle
- ☐ harem
- ☐ rainforest
- ☐ savanna
- ☐ territory
- ☐ waterfall

Vocabulary

▶ 下の語句の意味を調べ、表に記入しましょう。次に、英語の説明として適切なものを枠内から選び、記号で答えましょう。

語句	意味	説明
1. reproduce		
2. strive		
3. habitat		
4. exhibit		
5. induce		

語句	意味	説明
6. prompt		
7. crucial		
8. confine		
9. ensure		
10. oblige		

a. to make a great effort to do something or get something
b. to cause a state or condition
c. to produce young
d. to make certain that something happens
e. an object or collection of objects on public display
f. to do a favor for
g. to prevent someone from leaving or escaping
h. to make someone decide to do something
i. the natural home or environment of an animal or plant
j. extremely important

Reading Analysis

▶ 英文を読んで、問いに答えましょう。

1   The beavers at the Minnesota Zoo seem engaged in an unending task. Each week they fell scores of inch-thick young trees for their winter food supply. Each week zoo workers surreptitiously replace the downed trees, anchoring new ones in the iron holders so the animals can keep on cutting. Letting the beavers do what comes naturally has paid off: Minnesota is one of the few zoos to get them to **reproduce** in captivity. The chimps at the St. Louis Zoo also work for a living: they poke stiff pieces of hay into an anthill to scoop out the baby food and honey that curators hide inside. Instead of idly awaiting banana handouts, the chimps get to manipulate tools, just as they do in the wild. Last year, when 13 gorillas moved into Zoo Atlanta's new $4.5 million rain forest, they mated and formed families— a rarity among captives. "Zoos have changed from being mere menageries to being celebrations of life," says John Gwynne of the Bronx Zoo. "As the wild places get smaller, ❸ the role of zoos gets larger, which means intensifying the naturalness of the experience for both visitors and animals."

NOTES　fell「…を伐採する」　surreptitiously「こっそりと」　anchor「…を繋ぎとめる」　anthill「アリ塚」　scoop out …「…をかき出す」　curator「管理者、(動物園の)園長」　handout「施し物」　manipulate「…を手で巧みに使う」　rarity「稀なこと」　captive「捕らわれの動物」　menagerie「見世物の動物」　intensify「…を強める」

❶ John Gwynne 氏によれば、動物園はどのように変わってきたのでしょうか。また具体例として、どのようなことが紹介されていますか。

　　　動物園は＿＿＿＿＿＿＿＿＿＿＿＿＿から＿＿＿＿＿＿＿＿＿＿＿＿＿へと変わってきた。

　　　具体例：[Minnesota Zoo] ＿＿＿＿＿に、冬の食糧となる＿＿＿＿＿を伐らせる。

　　　　　　　[St. Louis Zoo] ＿＿＿＿＿に、＿＿＿＿＿を使って食糧を採らせる。

　　　　　　　[Zoo Atlanta] 動物園の中に熱帯雨林を再現して、13 頭の＿＿＿＿＿を移した。

❷ Minnesota Zoo と Zoo Atlanta で、動物を自然に近い状態に置くことによって得られた共通の成果は何でしょうか。

　　　飼育された状態で、＿＿＿＿＿＿＿＿＿＿＿＿＿＿＿＿＿＿＿＿＿＿。

❸ "the role of zoos gets larger" の意味として最も適切なものを選びましょう。

　　a. Zoos are getting bigger.
　　b. Zoos are becoming more important.
　　c. Wild places are getting smaller.

2

Naturalistic zoos are hardly new: animals liberated from concrete cages have been romping on Bronx savannas since 1941. But as species become extinct at a rate unparalleled since the Cretaceous era and 100 acres of tropical forests vanish every minute, zoos are **striving** to make their settings match their new role as keepers of the biological flame. ❹ <u>Since 1980 the nation's 143 accredited zoos and aquariums have spent more than \$1 billion on renovation and construction, much of it going to create **habitats** that immerse both animals and visitors in the sights, sounds, feel and smell of the wild.</u> Today's best **exhibits** reproduce not just the look but also ❺ <u>the function of a natural habitat</u>: they encourage the residents to mate, to raise young and to develop the survival skills they would need on the savannas of Africa or the slopes of the Andes....

3

Lately, curators have been making exhibits not only look real but ❻ <u>sound real</u>. At the Bronx Zoo's lush Jungle World the shrieks of gibbons, the cacophony of crickets and the trills of hornbills emanate from 65 speakers. The zoo's resident audio expert, Tom Veltre, spent a month in Thailand stringing microphones and a mile of cables up and down mountains to capture the sounds of the jungle. Even though the animals figure out that the hoots and howls are coming from black boxes, and not from furry or feathered neighbors, the call of the wild can shape their behavior. At Healesville Sanctuary, outside Melbourne, Australia, nighttime sounds cue nocturnal platypuses when to sleep, says bio-acoustician Leslie Gilbert; realistic noises also snap gorillas out of stress-**induced** lethargy.

NOTES romp「跳ね回る」 savanna「サバンナ」 Cretaceous「白亜紀」 accredited「公認の」 immerse「…を夢中にさせる」 lush「青々と茂った」 shriek「かん高い声」 gibbon「テナガザル」 cacophony「不協和音」 trill「震え声」 hornbill「サイチョウ」 emanate「…を発する」 hoot「ホーホーと鳴く音」 howl「遠吠え」 furry「毛皮の」 feathered「羽毛の生えた」 cue「…にきっかけを与える」 nocturnal「夜行性の」 platypus「カモノハシ」 bio-acoustician「生物音響学者」 ...-induced「…により引き起こされた」 lethargy「無気力」

❹ 急速な勢いで熱帯雨林が失われて種が絶滅している現在、動物園の新しい役割として、どのような取り組みが行われていますか。"Since ..." で始まる文を訳しましょう。

❺ "the function of a natural habitat" を再現することで期待できる成果を3つ、英語で挙げましょう。

- _____
- _____
- _____

❻ "sound real"とは、どのようなことでしょうか。Bronx ZooのJungle Worldの場合についてまとめましょう。

動物園の音響の専門家が、_____で1か月かけて録音した音（テナガザルのかん高い声、コオロギの耳障りな鳴き声、サイチョウのさえずり）を、動物園の____個のスピーカーから流した。動物たちは、それがスピーカーから流れているということを_____が、野生の声は_____。

❼ ❻の答えの他に、音の効果として期待できることを2つ、日本語で挙げましょう。

■ _____
■ _____

4

❽ "Natural" is now going beyond sight and sound to include everything from weather to activity patterns. Every day 11 rainstorms hit Tropic World at the Brookfield Zoo outside Chicago, **prompting** the monkeys to drop from their vines and scamper for cover amid cliffs, 50-foot-high gunite trees and 6,000 tropical plants. Regardless of the climate, the monkeys exhibit an array of behaviors never displayed in cages, such as rustling bushes to define their territories. At the San Diego Zoo's Sun Bear Forest, lion-tailed macaques are surrounded by jungle vines and cascading waterfalls. As soon as these highly endangered monkeys moved in last month, they fanned out and began foraging for fruit and other dainties left by the curators. They even respond to the dominant male's alarm call by clustering around him—something keepers had never seen. At Seattle's Woodland Park Zoo, elephants in the exhibit that opened last month roll and stack logs just as they do in a Thai logging camp. The task relieves the pachyderms' boredom.

5

Curators of rare species are focusing on how to induce one particular natural behavior—reproduction. At New York's Central Park Zoo, which reopened last year after a multimillion-dollar overhaul, the lights in the penguin house mimic seasonal changes in the austral day and night, which serve as a **crucial** cue for the birds' breeding cycle. At the San Diego Wild Animal Park, people are **confined** to cages (an electric monorail), and 2,600 animals roam free on 700 acres of veld and savanna. A white rhino that had never mated during 10 years at the San Diego Zoo has sired 55 offspring since moving into a 110-acre area at the park 17 years ago. "The difference is that he has room to mark out his territory and a harem [of 20] from which to choose," says spokesman Tom Hanscom. Getting flamingos to breed was simply a matter of providing more neighbors. For reasons curators cannot explain, the leggy pink birds never bred when they lived in two flocks of 50. But when merged into a group of 100 they began to build little mud mounds in the lake shallows on which to lay their eggs.

NOTES scamper「駆け回る」　gunite「グナイト：施工面に吹きつけるモルタル」　macaque「マカーク（ザル）」
cascade「滝のように落ちる」　forage「(食糧を)あさる、探し回る」　dainty「ごちそう」
pachyderm「(ゾウ、カバ、サイなどの)厚皮動物」　boredom「退屈」　overhaul「総点検」　mimic「…をまねる」
austral「南半球の」　roam「ぶらつく」　veld「広々とした草原」　rhino「サイ」(rhinoceros の口語)　sire「子をつくる」
offspring「子孫」　harem「ハーレム」　leggy「脚のひょろ長い」　merge ... into ~「…をまとめて～にする」

❽ "Natural" という語には、なぜ " " のマークが付いているのでしょうか。

❾ このブロック（❹と❺）で紹介されている、景色や音以外の「自然」な環境をつくる工夫とは何でしょうか。下の表の空欄を埋めて整理しましょう。

動物園	動物	工夫	結果・成果
Brookfield Zoo	サル	園内の Tropic World に＿＿＿＿＿＿＿＿＿＿＿＿＿＿＿＿。崖をつくり、高さ50フィートの人工の木や6千本の熱帯植物を植える。	サルたちは避難場所を求めて走り回る。＿＿＿＿＿＿＿＿＿＿＿＿＿＿ために木をカサカサ鳴らすといった行動をとる。
San Diego Zoo	マカークザル	Sun Bear Forest にジャングルのツタ、流れ落ちる滝を再現。	すぐに散らばって食糧をあさり始めた。支配的な雄ザルが警戒の叫び声をあげると、その雄ザルの＿＿＿＿＿＿＿＿＿＿＿＿といった行動をとる。
Woodland Park Zoo, Seattle	＿＿＿＿	丸太を転がしたり、積み上げたりさせる。	その作業が動物たちを＿＿＿＿＿＿＿＿＿＿＿＿＿＿。
＿＿＿＿＿＿＿＿	ペンギン	ペンギン舎の光を＿＿＿＿＿＿＿＿＿＿＿＿＿＿＿＿＿＿＿＿＿＿＿＿に合わせる。	鳥類の＿＿＿＿のサイクルにとって極めて重要なきっかけとなる。
Wild Animal Park, San Diego	2600頭の動物	人間はモノレールに乗り、動物たちが700エーカーの大草原を＿＿＿＿＿＿＿＿＿＿＿＿＿ようにする。	
San Diego Zoo	白サイ	110エーカーのエリアに移動。	その後17年間で、＿＿＿頭の子どもの父親となった。

❿ 白サイやフラミンゴの例が示すように、飼育されている状態で動物たちが繁殖をする条件とは何だと思われますか。

6

Once fiercely competitive, most American zoos now participate in species-survival programs, intricate dating games for animals living far apart. Coordinated by the American Association of Zoological Parks and Aquariums, the ⓐ SSP's rely on studbooks that keep track of zoo animals' age and ancestry, helping curators determine how to pair up males and females from member zoos to maintain the species' health and avoid inbreeding. Animals move back and forth between zoos to **ensure** the best genetic mix. Right now Indian rhinos from the Oklahoma City and National zoos are cozying up to the Bronx Zoo's female.

7

Without such programs, many species would be extinct. "Zoos are becoming the last hope for a number of endangered species," says Ronald Tilson of the Minnesota Zoo. Indeed, there are more Siberian tigers in America's zoos than on Russia's northern tundra. ⓑ <u>For all their breeding successes, though, zoos will become little more than Noah's arks if nature continues to give way to pavement.</u> That is why the new naturalistic settings are designed with people in mind, too. "Part of a zoo's reason for being is to inform the public of the marvelous things that occur on this planet," says Warren Thomas, director of the Los Angeles Zoo. "You do that by re-creating the environment that shaped these animals." In zoo parlance, it is called habitat immersion: getting visitors curious and excited about wild places and teaching them that ⓒ (   ) is the single greatest threat to wild animals today.

8

In the rare cases when animals bred in captivity do have an ancestral home to return to, ⓓ <u>zoos are trying to **oblige** them.</u> "The closer you come to mimicking nature in captivity, the easier that is," says primate curator Ann Baker of Brookfield. Already the Bronx Zoo has returned condors to the Andes. Scientists at the National Zoo in Washington taught a group of golden lion tamarins survival skills, such as how to forage and to heed warning calls, and have released 67 into a reserve near Rio de Janeiro since 1984. Although 35 died, others not only survived but mated; so far, the freed animals have produced 13 surviving offspring. The San Diego Park has returned 49 oryxes—rare antelopes—to Oman, Jordan and Israel, where the graceful creatures have bred successfully. Black-foot ferrets, which a few years ago had dwindled to only 17 in the wild, have proliferated to 125 in captivity, and scientists plan to release the animals into prairie-dog territories in the Great Plains in a few years.

NOTES fiercely「激しく」 intricate「複雑な」 studbook「血統台帳」 ancestry「血統」 inbreeding「近親交配」
cozy up to ...「…と親しくなる」 extinct「絶滅した」 tundra「ツンドラ」 Noah's ark「ノアの箱舟」 parlance「用語」
immersion「侵入」 primate「霊長類の動物」 condor「コンドル」 golden lion tamarin「ゴールデンライオンタマリン」
heed「…に注意を払う」 oryx「オリックス」 antelope「アンテロープ」 graceful「優美な」
black-foot ferret「クロアシイタチ」 dwindle「衰える」 proliferate「…を繁殖させる」 prairie-dog「プレーリードッグ」

⓫ SSPは何の略でしょうか。正式名称を本文から抜き出して、その内容をまとめましょう。

正式名称：＿＿＿＿＿＿＿＿＿＿＿＿＿＿＿＿＿＿＿＿＿＿＿＿＿＿＿＿

内容：＿＿＿＿＿＿＿＿＿＿＿＿＿＿＿＿＿＿＿＿＿＿＿＿＿＿＿＿＿＿

⓬ "For all ..."の文の内容に合うように、次の文章の空欄を埋めましょう。

Even though zoos are successful in (　　　　　　　　　), it does not solve the problems. Zoos will be (　　　　　) the samples of collective species if men continue to destroy (　　　　　　　　　) for animals and make the land into pavement.

⓭ 本文中の空欄に適する語句を記入しましょう。

⓮ "zoos are trying to oblige them."の意味として最も適切なものを選びましょう。また、成功例として紹介されている動物名を英語で挙げ、成功の判断基準を考えましょう。

　　a. Zoos want to return animals to their natural environment.
　　b. Zoos want to keep the animals in captivity.
　　c. Zoos are trying to get the animals to reproduce.

動物名：＿＿＿＿＿＿＿＿＿＿＿＿＿＿＿＿＿＿＿＿＿＿＿＿＿＿＿＿

基準：＿＿＿＿＿＿＿＿＿＿＿＿＿＿＿＿＿＿＿＿＿＿＿＿＿＿＿＿＿

9
2-16

With every animal that moves onto the endangered species list, or ⓯ <u>drops off it by extinction</u>, zoos assume greater importance. About 120 million people will visit U.S. zoos this year, giving curators 120 million chances to spread the conservation gospel. By showing how animals are shaped and supported by their environment, "zoos are trying to protect wild places as well as wild things," says Zoo Atlanta director Terry Maple. ⓰ <u>For as the wild places go, so go the wild animals.</u>

NOTES gospel「福音」

⓯ "drops off it by extinction"の意味として最も適切なものを選びましょう。

　　a. all die
　　b. survive
　　c. increase

⓰ "For as ..."の文と同じ意味になるように、次の文を完成させましょう。

When the animals' natural environment disappears, (　　　　　　　　　　　).

UNIT 3   THE ENVIRONMENT

Information Organization

▶ 下のアウトラインを使って、本文の主旨と内容を整理しましょう。空欄にあてはまる語を英語で記入しましょう。空欄に入る語は1語とは限りません。

Main Idea:

As many species of animals are being threatened with extinction, the role of zoos has become (1.   ). This role includes (2.   ) endangered animals and providing naturalistic settings to encourage the animals to (3.   ).

Details:

I. **Examples of Animal Behavior in Naturalistic Settings**
   A. Beavers cut down trees for their (4.   ).
   B. (5.   ) work for food by manipulating tools.
   C. Gorillas mate and (6.   ).

II. **Zoos Re-create Animals' Natural Environment**
   What zoos do: reproduce sights, (7.   ), smells, and feel of the wild
   Examples: rainstorms, cliffs, trees, plants, jungle vines, waterfalls, natural sounds, natural foods, artificial day and night
   Results: Animals mate, raise young, and develop (8.   )

III. **Species-Survival Programs (SSPs)**
   A. Purpose of the SSPs
      1. To pair up males and females from (9.   )
      2. To breed (10.   )
      3. To inform and excite the public about zoos and animals
   B. Examples of Successful (11.   ) into the Wild
      1. The return of condors to the Andes
      2. The release of golden lion tamarins (12.   ) in Brazil
      3. The return of oryxes to Oman, Jordan, and Israel

Short Summary

▶ 空欄に適する単語を記入して、本文全体の要約文を完成させましょう。

The role of zoos has become increasingly important as more animals are (1.   ) with extinction. Zoos have begun providing more (2.   ) settings, which encourage animals to (3.   ), and exchanging animals for breeding purposes. Zoos preserve (4.   ) animals and sometimes even (5.   ) them to their natural environments.

Critical Thinking

▶ 以下の質問について自分の意見をまとめましょう。そして、ペアやグループで話し合ったり、クラスで発表したりしましょう。

1. Compare the zoos in this country with zoos in your country and in other countries. How are they similar? How are they different?

2. Many zoo curators and other specialists are trying to save species of animals from extinction. Do you think it is important to try to preserve these animals?

CHAPTER 9

Antarctica: Whose Continent Is It Anyway?

Pre-reading Preparation

▶ あなたは南極大陸にどのようなイメージを持っていますか。南極大陸を描写する表現を次の中から選んでチェックしましょう（複数回答可）。

☐ deserted ☐ dry ☐ strong wind ☐ high mountain ☐ glacier
☐ grassy ☐ humid ☐ severely cold ☐ natural resources

Vocabulary

▶ 下の語句の意味を調べ、表に記入しましょう。次に、英語の説明として適切なものを枠内から選び、記号で答えましょう。

語句	意味	説明	語句	意味	説明
1. remote			6. dismiss		
2. treasure (v.)			7. primarily		
3. deprive			8. negotiate		
4. ruin (n.)			9. indication		
5. isolation			10. binding		

a. to prevent someone from having or using something
b. the state of being separated from other people
c. mostly; mainly
d. to keep something because you think it is very special
e. to talk about a problem or a situation in order to complete the arrangement
f. being far away from cities and places where most people live
g. involving an obligation that cannot be broken
h. the state of being severely damaged or spoiled
i. to say that it is not important enough for you to think about
j. a sign or piece of information that suggests something

Reading Analysis

▶ 英文を読んで、問いに答えましょう。

1 🎧 2-17

Last February, the World Discoverer, our cruise ship, stopped in front of a white ice cliff higher than the ship's mast. As large as France, the Ross Ice Shelf of Antarctica extends unbroken along the Ross Sea for hundreds of miles.

2 🎧 2-18

Like other passengers on our cruise ship, we had been lured by ❷ an irresistible attraction: the chance to visit the most **remote** place on Earth, and the most unusual. The coldest place on Earth is also the subject of conflicting interests: scientists, tourists, environmentalists, oil and mineral seekers.

3 🎧 2-19

Scientists **treasure** the unparalleled advantages for research; tourists prize the chance to visit Earth's last frontier; environmentalists fear that increases in both activities will pollute the continent and jeopardize its fabulous creatures; ❹ others contend that preserving Antarctica as a kind of world park will **deprive** the rest of the world of much needed oil and mineral reserves.

4 🎧 2-20

Fears of Antarctica's **ruin** through commercial exploitation have been partly reduced by the October, 1991, 31-nation signing of ❺ the Madrid Protocol, which bans oil and gas exploration for the next 50 years. But Antarctica's unique attributes—it is the coldest, driest, and highest continent—will keep it at the focus of conflicting scientific and touristic interests.

NOTES　lure「…を引きつける」　irresistible「抑えがたい」　unparalleled「無類の」　pollute「…を汚染する」
jeopardize「…を危険にさらす」　fabulous「素晴らしい」　contend「…を強く主張する」　reserves「埋蔵量」
exploitation「開発」　the Madrid Protocol「マドリッド議定書（南極条約議定書）」　attribute「特性」

❶ 第1パラグラフの内容をまとめましょう。

_____は去年2月にWorld Discovererという_____で_____を訪問した。Ross Ice Shelfはフランスと_____があり、Ross Sea沿岸に何百マイルも_____。

❷ "an irresistible attraction"の具体的な内容を述べている箇所に波下線（～～）を引き、その内容を日本語でまとめましょう。

内容：_____

UNIT 3　THE ENVIRONMENT

❸ 次のそれぞれの立場の人たちの南極大陸に対する見解をまとめましょう。

科学者：＿＿＿＿＿＿＿＿＿＿＿＿＿＿＿＿＿＿＿＿＿＿＿＿＿＿＿＿と考えて大事にしている。

観光客：＿＿＿＿＿＿＿＿＿＿＿＿＿＿＿＿＿＿と考えて珍重している。

環境保護論者：＿＿＿＿＿＿＿＿＿＿＿＿＿＿＿＿＿の活発化によって、南極が汚染され、＿＿＿＿
＿＿＿＿＿＿＿＿＿＿＿＿＿＿＿＿＿＿＿＿だろうと恐れている。

その他：南極を＿＿＿＿＿＿＿＿＿＿＿＿＿＿＿として保護したならば、世界のその他の地域から
＿＿＿＿＿＿＿＿＿＿＿＿＿＿＿＿＿＿＿＿＿＿＿＿＿を奪うことになると主張する。

❹ "others" が指す語句を第1～3パラグラフから抜き出しましょう。

＿＿＿＿＿＿＿＿＿＿＿＿＿＿＿＿＿＿＿＿＿＿＿＿＿

❺ "the Madrid Protocol" についてまとめましょう。

■ 1991年10月、＿＿＿か国が調印。

■ 今後50年間、南極大陸における＿＿＿＿＿＿＿＿＿＿＿＿＿＿＿＿＿＿＿＿＿＿。

■ その結果、＿＿＿＿＿＿＿＿＿＿＿＿＿＿＿＿＿＿＿＿＿＿＿＿＿はある程度軽減された。

5

2-21

　　Think of a place as remote as the far side of the moon, as strange as Saturn and as inhospitable as Mars, and ❻that will give some idea of what Antarctica is like. A mere 2.4 percent of its 5.4 million-square-mile land mass is ice-free, and then, only for a few months a year. Scientists estimate that 70 percent of the world's fresh water is locked away in Antarctica's icecap; if it were ever to melt, sea levels might rise 200 feet. In Antarctica, winds can blow at better than 200 mph, and temperatures drop as low as minus 128.6°F. There is not a single village or town, not a tree, bush, or blade of grass on the entire continent.

NOTES　inhospitable「荒涼として」　icecap「氷冠」　minus 128.6°F「華氏－128.6度＝約摂氏－89.2度」　blade「葉」

❻ "that" の具体的な内容を述べている箇所に波下線を引き、その内容を日本語で答えましょう。

内容：＿＿＿
＿＿

❼ 南極大陸の特徴をまとめましょう。

■ 全面積＿＿＿＿＿＿＿＿＿＿＿＿＿＿のうち＿＿＿＿＿＿＿＿＿＿＿＿＿＿＿＿割合は2.4%
のみで、それも1年のうち＿＿＿＿＿＿＿のみ。

■ ＿＿＿＿＿＿＿＿の70%が南極の＿＿＿＿＿＿＿＿＿＿＿＿＿＿＿＿＿＿＿＿＿＿＿＿＿。

■ 万一、南極の＿＿＿＿＿＿＿＿＿＿＿ならば、海水面が200フィート＿＿＿＿＿＿＿＿＿＿＿。

CHAPTER 9　Antarctica: Whose Continent Is It Anyway?

- ■ ＿＿＿＿はゆうに時速 200 マイルを超えることがある。
- ■ ＿＿＿＿は華氏マイナス 128.6 度まで下がる。
- ■ 大陸全域に＿＿＿＿＿＿は 1 つもなく、＿＿＿＿＿＿は 1 本も生えていない。

6
2-22

　But far from being merely a useless continent, ❽ Antarctica is vital to life on Earth. The continent's vast ice fields reflect sunlight back into space, preventing the planet from overheating. The cold water that the breakaway icebergs generate flows north and mixes with equatorial warm water, producing currents, clouds, and ultimately creating complex weather patterns. Antarctic seas teem with life, making them an important link in the world ❾ food chain. The frigid waters of the Southern Ocean are home to species of birds and mammals that are found nowhere else.

7
2-23

　The National Science Foundation (NSF) is the government agency responsible for the U.S. stations in Antarctica. Because of the continent's extreme cold and almost complete **isolation**, the NSF considers it to be the best place to study and understand such phenomena as temperature circulation in the oceans, unique animal life, ozone depletion, and glacial history. And buried deep in layers of Antarctic ice lie clues to ancient climates, clues such as trapped bubbles of atmospheric gases, which can help predict whether present and future global warming poses a real threat.

8
2-24

　Until scientists began the first serious study of the continent during the 1957–58 International Geophysical Year (IGY), a multicountry cooperative research project, Antarctica was **dismissed** as a vast, useless continent.

NOTES　equatorial「赤道付近の」　ultimately「最終的に」　teem with ...「…で満ちあふれている」　frigid「極寒の」
the Southern Ocean「南極海」　the National Science Foundation「アメリカ国立科学財団」
ozone depletion「オゾン層破壊」　glacial「氷河の」　the International Geophysical Year「国際地球観測年」

❽ "Antarctica is vital to life on Earth." の具体例を表す内容を 4 点にまとめて日本語で説明しましょう。

1. ＿＿＿＿＿＿＿＿＿＿＿＿＿＿＿＿＿＿＿＿＿＿＿＿＿＿＿＿＿＿＿＿＿＿＿＿
2. ＿＿＿＿＿＿＿＿＿＿＿＿＿＿＿＿＿＿＿＿＿＿＿＿＿＿＿＿＿＿＿＿＿＿＿＿
　＿＿＿＿＿＿＿＿＿＿＿＿＿＿＿＿＿＿＿＿＿＿＿＿＿＿＿＿＿＿＿＿＿＿＿＿
3. ＿＿＿＿＿＿＿＿＿＿＿＿＿＿＿＿＿＿＿＿＿＿＿＿＿＿＿＿＿＿＿＿＿＿＿＿
4. ＿＿＿＿＿＿＿＿＿＿＿＿＿＿＿＿＿＿＿＿＿＿＿＿＿＿＿＿＿＿＿＿＿＿＿＿

87

❾ "food chain" の例として最も適切なものを選びましょう。

　　a. algae（藻） → salmon → bears
　　b. insects → birds → fish
　　c. farmer → supermarket → people

❿ The National Science Foundation が南極大陸で行っている調査・研究にはどのようなものがあるでしょうか。また、それらを南極大陸で行うのはなぜでしょうか。

　調査・研究の対象：＿＿＿＿＿＿＿＿＿＿＿＿＿＿＿＿＿＿＿＿＿＿＿＿＿＿＿＿＿＿＿＿

　理由：＿＿＿＿＿＿＿＿＿＿＿＿＿＿＿＿＿＿＿＿＿＿＿＿＿＿＿＿＿＿＿＿＿＿＿＿＿＿

⓫ 第8パラグラフの内容に合うように、次の文章の空欄を埋めましょう。

The International Geophysical Year was an (　　　　　　　　) scientific project that lasted from 1957 to 1958. Scientists (　　　　　　) the first serious study of Antarctica during the IGY. (　　　　　　) the IGY, Antarctica was thought of as a useless continent.

9

　　Based upon early explorations and questionable land grants, seven countries, including Great Britain, Chile, and Argentina, claim sovereignty over vast tracts of the continent. However, as IGY wound down, the question of who owns Antarctica came to a head. The 12 participating countries reached an international agreement, the Antarctic Treaty, which took effect in June 1961. The number has since grown, making 39 in all. It established Antarctica as a "continent for science and peace," and temporarily set aside all claims of sovereignty for as long as the treaty remains in effect.

10

　　The rules of the treaty meant that as tourists to Antarctica, passengers on our cruise ship needed neither passports nor visas. Except for a handful of sites of special scientific interest, specially protected areas, and specially managed areas, there was nothing to restrict us from wandering anywhere we wanted.

11

　　Primarily because of its scientific and ecological importance, many scientists feel that Antarctica should be dedicated to research only. They feel that tourists should not be permitted to come. However, recent events have shown that the greatest future threat to Antarctica may not be tourism or scientific stations, but the worldwide thirst for oil and minerals. "The reason the Antarctic Treaty was **negotiated** and went through so quickly," geologist John Splettstoesser explains, "is that at the time, relatively few minerals were known to exist there."

12   By the early 1970s, however, there were some **indications** that there might be gas and oil in Antarctica. The treaty countries decided that no commercial companies would be permitted to explore for resources. The Madrid Protocol bans all exploration or commercial exploitation of natural resources on the continent for the next 50 years.

> **NOTES**   land grant「土地供与」 sovereignty「統治権」 tract「区画」 wound down > wind down「終わりに近づく」
> the Antarctic Treaty「南極条約」 take effect「(法律などが)効力を発する」 ecological「生態学上の」
> dedicate「…をささげる」 thirst「渇望」 geologist「地質学者」

❶❷ IGYが終わりに近づくと、注目されるようになったことは何でしょうか。第9パラグラフから抜き出しましょう。

_____

❶❸ the Antarctic Treatyについてまとめましょう。

12か国が同意し1961年に_____、のちに参加国は___か国に拡大した。条約では南極大陸を_____と定め、条約が失効するまでは_____を当面は無効とするもの。

❶❹ John Splettstoesserによると、当時条約が素早くまとまった理由は何でしょうか、それを表している箇所を抜き出し、日本語で説明しましょう。

箇所：_____

理由：_____

UNIT 3   THE ENVIRONMENT

Like the Antarctic Treaty itself, the Madrid Protocol is **binding** only on the 39 treaty countries. There is nothing to stop non-treaty countries from establishing commercial bases anywhere on the continent and doing whatever they please.

Where do we go from here? So far, no non-treaty nation has expressed a serious interest in setting up for business in Antarctica. So far, ⑮ none of the countries claiming sovereignty has moved to formally annex Antarctic territory.

So whose continent is Antarctica, anyway? Former Vice President Albert Gore best expresses the feelings of those of us who have fallen in love with this strange and spectacular land: ⑯ "I think that it should be held in trust as a global ecological reserve for all the people of the world, not just in this generation, but later generations to come as well."

NOTES   annex「…を併合する」   Albert Gore「アルバート・ゴア：米国元副大統領、環境活動家」   in trust「信託して」

⑮ "none of the countries claiming sovereignty ..." で始まる文は何を意味しているでしょうか。下から1つ選びましょう。

   a. Not a single country has moved to make Antarctica part of its own country.
   b. Few countries have moved to set up government in Antarctica.
   c. No countries have sent a number of people to settle in Antarctica

⑯ "I think that it should be held ..." で始まる Albert Gore の発言を訳しましょう。筆者はなぜこの発言を引用したと思いますか。その理由を考えましょう。

訳：＿＿＿

＿＿＿

理由：＿＿

＿＿＿

Information Organization

▶ 下のアウトラインを使って、本文の内容を整理しましょう。空欄にあてはまる語を英語で記入しましょう。空欄に入る語は1語とは限りません。

I. People with Conflicting Interests in Antarctica
　A. Scientist
　　Reason: They (1. _____) for research.
　B. Tourists
　　Reason: They prize the chance to visit Earth's (2. _____).
　C. Environmentalists
　　Reason: They fear that increases in research and tourism will jeopardize Antarctica.
　D. (3. _____)
　　Reason: They contend that the world will be deprived of natural resources if Antarctica is not exploited.

II. (4. _____)
　A. date: October, 1991
　B. original number of (5. _____): 31
　C. purpose: (6. _____) oil and gas exploitation for 50 years

III. A Description of Antarctica
　A. Only 2.4 % of its 5.4 million-square-mile land mass is (7. _____).
　B. 70 % of the world's (8. _____) is trapped in its icecap.
　C. Winds can blow at more than 200 mph, and temperatures drop to minus 128.6°F.
　D. There are no villages, towns, or plants.

IV. Antarctica Is (9. _____) **on Earth.**
　A. It reflects sunlight back into space, (10. _____) Earth from overheating.
　B. Cold water from icebergs produces currents, clouds, and creates complex weather patterns.
　C. Antarctic seas are an important link in the world (11. _____).
　D. The Southern Ocean is home to unique animals.

V. (12. _____) **Purpose**
　A. Establish Antarctica as a "continent for science and peace"
　B. Temporarily set aside all claims of sovereignty
　C. Open to all: People need (13. _____).

Short Summary

▶ 空欄に適する単語を記入して、本文全体の要約文を完成させましょう。

Although no one (¹.   ) on Antarctica and no nation (².   ) ownership of it, many groups of people have conflicting (³.   ) in studying and exploiting it. Treaties have been (⁴.   ) by many nations to protect Antarctica—a cold, icy, (⁵.   ) continent.

Critical Thinking

▶ 以下の質問について自分の意見をまとめましょう。そして、ペアやグループで話し合ったり、クラスで発表したりしましょう。

1. The authors ask who Antarctica belongs to. Whose continent is Antarctica? Do you think it should belong to one country, many countries, or to no one? Why do you think so?

2. In Paragraph 5, the authors describe Antarctica by comparing it with other places and by giving facts about it. The authors are trying to convey an image and a feeling about this unusual continent. Imagine that you are visiting Antarctica and describe what you see and how being in Antarctica makes you feel.

UNIT 4

ETHICAL ISSUES

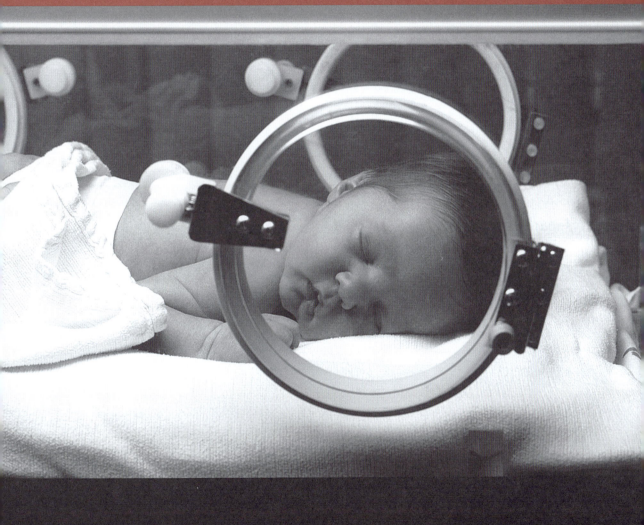

CHAPTER 10

Matters of Life and Death

Pre-reading Preparation

▶ あなたは尊厳死について、どのように考えますか。あなたの立場に最も近いものを次の中から選んでチェックしましょう。

☐ strongly disagree ☐ disagree ☐ agree when they suffer too much pain
☐ agree only when there is no hope for a cure ☐ strongly agree

Vocabulary

▶ 下の語句の意味を調べ、表に記入しましょう。次に、英語の説明として適切なものを枠内から選び、記号で答えましょう。

語句	意味	説明	語句	意味	説明
1. privilege			6. reverse (n.)		
2. controversial			7. appreciation		
3. formerly			8. fatal		
4. artificial			9. coincidence		
5. surgeon			10. reasonable		

a. made or produced by human beings, for example using science or technology
b. being the subject of intense public argument, disagreement, or disapproval
c. causing death; deadly
d. the opposite to that previously stated
e. a doctor who is specially trained to perform operation
f. having sound judgement; fair and sensible
g. your thanks for something that someone does for you
h. a special right or advantage that only one person or group has
i. when two or more similar events occur at the same time by chance
j. in the past; in earlier times

Reading Analysis

▶ 英文を読んで、問いに答えましょう。

1 〔2-32〕

In a new book, *A Miracle and a **Privilege***, Dr. Francis Moore, 81, of Harvard Medical School, discusses a lifetime of grappling with the issue of when to help a patient die. An excerpt:

2 〔2-33〕

Doctors of our generation are not newcomers to ❷ this question. Going back to my internship days, I can remember many patients in pain, sometimes in a coma or delirious, with late, hopeless cancer. For many of ❸ them, we wrote an order for heavy medication—morphine by the clock. This was not talked about openly and little was written about it. ❹ It was essential, not **controversial**.

NOTES grapple with ...「…に取り組む」 excerpt「抜粋」 newcomer「新参者」 coma「昏睡状態」 delirious「せん妄状態の」 morphine「モルヒネ：疼痛を緩和する麻薬の一種（大量摂取は死に至る）」 by the clock「規則的な間隔で」

❶ 新刊 *A Miracle and a Privilege* の内容は何でしょうか。

Dr. Moore が、＿＿＿＿＿＿＿＿＿＿＿＿＿＿＿＿＿＿＿＿＿＿＿＿＿＿＿＿＿＿＿＿

＿＿＿＿＿＿＿＿＿＿＿＿＿＿＿＿＿＿＿＿＿＿＿＿＿＿＿＿＿＿を考察している。

❷ "this question" が指す内容を本文から抜き出しましょう。

＿＿＿＿＿＿＿＿＿＿＿＿＿＿＿＿＿＿＿＿＿＿＿＿＿＿＿＿＿＿＿＿＿＿＿＿＿

❸ "them" が指す内容を日本語で答えましょう。

＿＿＿＿＿＿＿＿＿＿＿＿＿＿＿＿＿＿＿＿＿＿＿＿＿＿＿＿＿＿＿＿＿＿＿＿＿

❹ "It was essential, not controversial." の内容に合うように、次の文章の空欄を埋めましょう。

Giving terminal cancer patients heavy medication to help them (＿＿＿＿＿＿) without pain was necessary. It was not something people (＿＿＿＿＿＿) about.

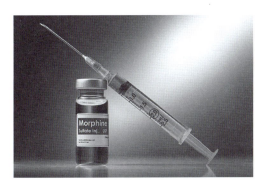

UNIT 4 ETHICAL ISSUES

3
2-34

The best way to bring the problem into focus is to describe two patients whom I cared for. The first, **formerly** a nurse, had sustained a fractured pelvis in an automobile accident. A few days later her lungs seemed to fill up; her urine stopped; her heart developed dangerous rhythm disturbances. So there she was: in a coma, on dialysis, on a breathing machine, her heartbeat maintained with an electrical device. One day after rounds, my secretary said the husband and son of the patient wanted to see me. They told me their wife and mother was obviously going to die; she was a nurse and had told her family that she never wanted this kind of terrible death, being maintained by machines. I told them that while I respected their view, there was nothing intrinsically lethal about her situation. The kidney failure she had was just the kind for which the **artificial** kidney was most effective. ❼ <u>While possibly a bit reassured, they were disappointed.</u> Here was the head **surgeon**, seemingly determined to keep everybody alive, ❽ (   ).

4
2-35

When patients start to get very sick, they often seem to fall apart all at once. ❾ <u>The **reverse** is also true.</u> Within a few days, the patient's pacemaker could be removed, and she awoke from her coma. About six months later I was again in my office. ❿ <u>The door opened and in walked a gloriously fit woman.</u> After some cheery words of **appreciation**, the father and son asked to speak to me alone. As soon as the door closed, both men became quite tearful. All that came out was, "We want you to know how wrong we were."

NOTES sustain「…を被る、負う」 fractured pelvis「骨盤骨折」 urine「尿」 rhythm disturbance「(心)律動障害」
dialysis「透析」 round「回診」 intrinsically「本質的に」 lethal「致死の」 kidney failure「腎不全」
pacemaker「ペースメーカー」 gloriously「光り輝いて」 cheery「陽気な」

❺ 最初の患者の症状についてまとめましょう。

　　　_____で骨盤を骨折し、数日後、肺は塞がったようになり、尿は止まり、心臓は危険な律動障害を起こしていた。_____状態で、透析を続け、_____につながれて、心拍は_____によって維持されていた。

❻ 患者の家族からの依頼に対するDr. Mooreの返答に波下線（～～）を引き、その部分を訳しましょう。

訳：_____

❼ "While possibly a bit reassured, they were disappointed." について、彼らが安心した点と失望した点を答えましょう。

安心した点：_____

失望した点：_____

_____

❽ 本文中の空欄に最も適切な語句を下から選び、記入しましょう。

[no matter what / if possible / by chance / no longer]

❾ "The reverse is also true." の意味に合うように、次の文の空欄を埋めましょう。

It means that patients can (　　　　　　　　) from a serious condition quickly, too.

❿ "The door opened ..." で始まる文は倒置文です。なぜ筆者は倒置文や副詞 gloriously を使ったのでしょうか。その理由を考えましょう。

_____

_____

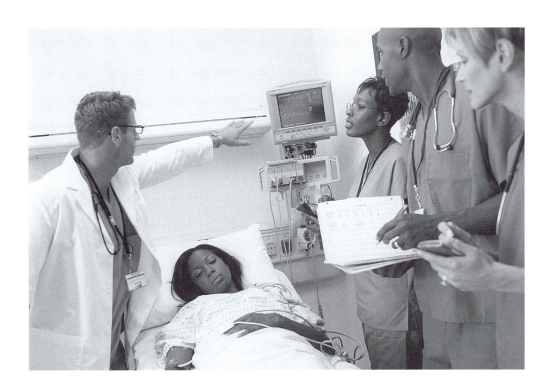

5

The second patient was an 85-year-old lady whose hair caught fire while she was smoking. She arrived with a deep burn; ⓫ <u>I knew it would surely be **fatal**</u>. As a remarkable **coincidence**, there was a seminar going on at the time in medical ethics, given by the wife of an official of our university. She asked me if I had any sort of ethical problem I could bring up for discussion. I described ⓬ <u>the case</u> and asked the students their opinion. After the discussion, I made a remark that was, in retrospect, a serious mistake. I said, "I'll take the word back to the nurses about her, and we will talk about it some more before we decide." The instructor and the students were shocked: "You mean this is a real patient?" The teacher of ethics was not accustomed to being challenged by reality. In any event, I went back and met with the nurses. A day or two later, when she was making no progress and was suffering terribly, we began to back off treatment. When she complained of pain, we gave her plenty of morphine. A great plenty. Soon she died quietly and not in pain. As a **reasonable** physician, you had better move ahead and do what you would want done for you. And ⓭ <u>do not discuss it with the world first</u>. There is a lesson here for everybody. Assisting people to leave this life requires strong judgment and long experience to avoid its misuse.

NOTES deep burn「Ⅲ度熱傷：度数は火傷の深さを示す」　ethics「倫理学」　ethical「倫理上の」　in retrospect「思い返せば」
be accustomed to ...「…に慣れている」　physician「医師」　misuse「誤用、乱用」

⓫ "I knew it would surely be fatal."は何を意味しているでしょうか。下から1つ選びましょう。

　a. The doctor thought the patient might live.

　b. The doctor thought the patient might die.

　c. The doctor knew the patient would die.

⓬ "the case"を具体的に描写しましょう。

＿＿歳の女性、＿＿＿＿＿＿＿＿＿＿＿＿＿＿ときに火が髪の毛に燃え移り、Ⅲ度熱傷で入院。患者が＿＿＿＿＿＿＿＿＿＿＿＿＿＿ということがわかっている事例。

⓭ ⓬の患者への対応の経過を整理しましょう。

致命的だと判断した　→　看護師と対応を相談する　→　患者には＿＿＿＿＿＿が見られない　→　積極的な＿＿＿＿＿＿を止める　→　患者が＿＿＿＿＿を訴える　→　＿＿＿＿＿＿＿＿＿＿＿＿＿＿＿　→　患者が静かに息を引き取る

⑭ "do not discuss it with the world first." は何を意味しているでしょうか。下から1つ選びましょう。

    a. Do not talk about your patients at seminars.
    b. Do not talk about your patients with nurses.
    c. Do not talk to many people about your patients.

⑮ the issue of when to help a patient die に関して、Dr. Moore の結論となる2文に波下線を引き、その内容を日本語でまとめましょう。

内容：_____

_____

_____

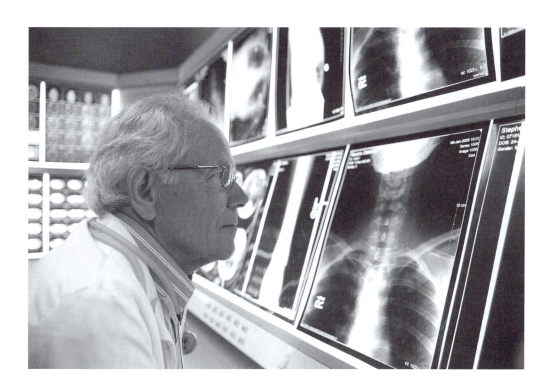

UNIT 4　ETHICAL ISSUES

Information Organization

▶ 下のフローチャートを使って、本文の内容を整理しましょう。空欄にあてはまる語を英語で記入しましょう。空欄に入る語は1語とは限りません。

The Dilemma
For doctors with terminally ill patients, the dilemma is whether to actively help these patients (1.   ).

Case #1
A former (2.   ) who had sustained a fractured pelvis. Her condition was serious: her lungs filled up; her urine stopped, her heart (3.   ) dangerous rhythm disturbances. She was on life support equipment. Her family (4.   ) that the doctor take her off the machines.

Case #2
An 85-year-old woman whose hair caught fire. Her condition: she had a deep burn and her condition was probably (7.   ).

Dr. Moore's Decision
He decided not to take her off the (5.   ).

Dr. Moore's Decision
They backed off treatment; they gave her (8.   ).

Outcome
She (6.   ) and left the hospital.

Outcome
She died (9.   ) in the hospital.

The Lesson of Dr. Moore's Experience
As a reasonable (10.   ), you should do what you would want done for you. Assisting people to die requires (11.   ) and (12.   ) to avoid its misuse.

Short Summary

▶ 空欄に適する単語を記入して、本文全体の要約文を完成させましょう。

Dr. Moore, 81, has practiced medicine all his life. He describes two very ill (¹.   ) he treated differently. One he refused to let (².   ); the other he did help die. He brought up the second patient's case at an (³.   ) seminar, where the participants were surprised that he discussed a real case taking place in the present day. In both cases, he feels he made the right (⁴.   ). He believes that the decision to help end a patient's life requires strong (⁵.   ) and long experience.

Critical Thinking

▶ 以下の質問について自分の意見をまとめましょう。そして、ペアやグループで話し合ったり、クラスで発表したりしましょう。

1. In the United States, some people write a "living will" before their death. A "living will" can prevent doctors from prolonging a person's life if he or she becomes seriously ill. Would you want to write a "living will"? If so, under what conditions would you want to be allowed to die naturally? If not, why not?

2. If someone you loved were terminally ill and wanted his or her doctor to perform an assisted suicide, would you approve? Would you encourage the doctor to agree to assist in the suicide?

CHAPTER 11

Switched at Birth:
Women Learn the Truth 56 Years Later

Pre-reading Preparation

▶ もしあなたに兄弟や姉妹がいると仮定した場合、どのようなところが似てくると思いますか。次の中から選んでチェックしましょう（複数回答可）。

☐ body structure ☐ eye or hair color ☐ face form ☐ gesture
☐ personality   ☐ taste   ☐ values   ☐ voice

Vocabulary

▶ 下の語句の意味を調べ、表に記入しましょう。次に、英語の説明として適切なものを枠内から選び、記号で答えましょう。

語句	意味	説明	語句	意味	説明
1. intuition			6. clan		
2. cheat			7. suspicion		
3. uneventful			8. biological		
4. undeniable			9. revelation		
5. alleged			10. sue		

- a. supposed to be true, but not having been proven
- b. relating to the natural processes performed by living things
- c. a large family, including aunts, cousins etc.
- d. to trick or deceive someone who trusts you
- e. the ability to understand something from your feelings rather than facts
- f. a surprising and previously unknown fact that has been disclosed to others
- g. to make a legal claim against someone because they have harmed you
- h. feeling that you do not like or trust someone or something
- i. definitely true or certain
- j. with nothing exciting or unusual happening

Reading Analysis

▶ 英文を読んで、問いに答えましょう。

1

When Oregon nurses handed Marjorie Angell her newborn daughter in the hospital in 1953, she insisted they had given her the wrong child. Her concerns were brushed off, but in an unlikely story that was 56 years in the making, her mother's **intuition** foreshadowed what was to come.

2

It was true. Her daughter had been switched at birth when she and the other baby were being bathed, but Marjorie Angell would never learn the truth because she died before it was revealed. "It's sad," DeeAnn Angell Schafer told "Good Morning America." "Just to think I missed out on knowing my own parents." Even though Kay Rene Reed Qualls said she enjoyed a wonderful life, she still feels guilty about the memories that should belong to DeeAnn and her family. "I look at them and I feel like I **cheated** somebody," she said. The story of two women who grew up in the wrong families just came to light last month to the surprise of everyone and no one.

NOTES　brush off …「…を無視する、はねつける」　foreshadow「…の前兆となる」

❶ 第1パラグラフの中から第2パラグラフの展開を予測させる部分を抜き出しましょう。

_____

❷ DeeAnn Angell SchaferとKay Rene Reed Qualls のどちらが、より強い衝撃を感じたと思われますか。また、どこからそれがわかるでしょうか。

_____
_____
_____

A Secret Switch?

On May 3, 1953, DeeAnn Angell of Fossil, Oregon, and Kay Rene Reed of Condon, Oregon, were born at Pioneer Memorial Hospital in the eastern Oregon town of Heppner. They grew up, got married, and had children and grandchildren of their own. The women's lives were **uneventful** until last summer, when Kay Rene's brother, Bobby Reed, received a call from an 86-year-old woman who claimed to hold ❸ an astonishing secret. He met the woman in her nursing home. She said she had known the Reeds' mother and had lived next door to the Angell family in Fossil. Her shocking claim was that Kay Rene was not really a Reed at all; she was an Angell. The elderly woman said Kay Rene and DeeAnn were switched at birth. To bolster her story, she showed Bobby Reed an old photo of DeeAnn's sister. Reed saw an instant and **undeniable** resemblance to the woman raised as his sister.

NOTES switch「交換する、取り替える」 Fossil「ファスル：米国オレゴン州ウィラー郡の郡庁所在地」
Condon「コンドン：米国オレゴン州ギリアム郡の郡庁所在地」 nursing home「老人ホーム」 bolster「…を強める」

❸ "an astonishing secret"の内容を考えましょう。

　Kay Reneは＿＿＿＿＿＿の人間ではない。＿＿＿＿＿＿の人間である。

❹ なぜこの老婦人は、秘密に気づいたのでしょうか。推測してみましょう。

　老婦人はReed家の＿＿＿＿＿＿＿＿いて、なおかつ＿＿＿＿＿＿の隣に住んでいた。そのため、＿＿＿＿＿＿の顔が＿＿＿＿＿＿＿の母と似ていて、彼女自身の姉妹とは＿＿＿＿＿＿＿と気づいたものと推測できる。だから、DeeAnnの姉妹の＿＿＿＿＿をBobbyに見せたのではないか。それが＿＿＿＿＿＿＿＿＿＿に似ていたので、さらに信憑性が増した。

4 🎧2-40   If what the elderly woman said was correct, then DeeAnn really was Reed's sister and not Kay Rene. The secret stunned Reed, who was unsure what to do with the ❺ potential bombshell. He always had known and loved Kay Rene as his sister. Though Kay Rene was a brunette in a sea of blonds, no one ever thought to question her paternity.

5 🎧2-41   Reed did not want anything to change, nor did he want to hurt anyone. He decided to tell his two oldest sisters, and one of them broke the news to Kay Rene. With both the Reed parents and the Angell parents dead, the children had to come together to uncover the truth about the **alleged** mix-up.

6 🎧2-42   The families learned rumors of babies being switched at birth had been around for decades. In fact, Kay Rene first learned of such gossip in 1995 when her sister Carol told her during their dying father's last camping trip. After his death, Kay Rene's mother approached her about the subject. She acknowledged that she heard another new mother in the same hospital, where she had given birth, question if her baby was her own. But after looking into Kay Rene's big brown eyes, she determined this was her baby and she would not bring the issue up anymore.

NOTES   stun「…をぼう然とさせる」 bombshell「爆弾」
brunette「ブルネット：髪がダークブラウンで、肌や目が黒または褐色の白人女性（男性は brunet）」 a sea of ...「豊かな…」
paternity「出生」 mix-up「取り違え」 bring ... up「…を持ち出す」

❺ "potential bombshell" とは、どのような意味でしょうか。あてはまるものを下から１つ選びましょう。

　a. Kay Rene was not really his sister.
　b. DeeAnn was not really his sister.
　c. Kay Rene looked different from her family.

❻ なぜ "potential bombshell" のような表現を使っているのでしょうか。

たとえば、この問題が＿＿＿＿になると、家族の中でいろいろなことが＿＿＿＿＿しまい、＿＿＿＿人も出てくる＿＿＿＿があるため。

❼ Reed 家の母親が、かつてこの問題について疑問を感じたと思いますか。[ ]内の自分の推測に合うほうを○で囲みましょう。そして、その答えがわかる箇所に波下線（〰〰）を引き、訳しましょう。

自分の推測：[疑問を感じた / 疑問を感じなかった]

訳：＿＿＿＿＿＿＿＿＿＿＿＿＿＿＿＿＿＿＿＿＿＿＿＿＿＿＿＿＿＿

UNIT 4 ETHICAL ISSUES

[_____]

7
🎧 2-43

Growing up, Kay Rene had questioned whether she truly was a Reed. She had her **⁸**( ). She knew she did not look like anyone else in her family. Eventually, Kay Rene said, the rumors started in her family that maybe she was not really related to them.

"I think all the older sisters knew this," she said. But neither woman ever had blood tests and DNA testing was not an option.

8
🎧 2-44

The doubts just lingered. Even Kay Rene's husband joked about whether the Reeds truly were her relatives after seeing her at family functions. Kay Rene just knew she did not want those thoughts to be true. **⁹** <u>She chalked them up to being ornery.</u> She justified her placement in the Reed **clan** by saying her blue eyes came from her father. DeeAnn, too, had **suspicions** growing up. She wondered why she loved horses so much. She received a phone call from her sister in February to tell her about the news—the rumors might be true.

NOTES linger「なかなか消えない、とどまっている」 function「行事」 chalk up ...「…を心にとどめる」 ornery「強情な、怒りっぽい」

❽ 本文中の空欄に適切なほうを [ ] 内から選び、記入しましょう。また、その根拠を説明しましょう。

[suspicions / ideas]

説明：_____

_____

❾ なぜ Kay Rene が "She chalked them up to being ornery." の状態になったと思いますか。考えてみましょう。

家族：似ていないので、_____かもしれないと言い出した。

姉　：みんな_____と思うが、_____を調べるとは言わなかった。

___：家族の間の行事で彼女の親兄弟に会った後、本当に家族なのかと_____を言った。

❿ DeeAnn はどんなことを疑問に思っていたでしょうか。またそこから、どのようなことが考えられるでしょうか。

疑問：_____

考えられること：_____

106

9 2-45

Kay Rene wanted to know the truth; she needed to know it. So last month, she, her brother and their sister Dorothy met the blond-haired DeeAnn at a Kennewick, Washington, clinic for a DNA test. When Kay Rene finally met the Angell family, she realized she looked more like them. ⓫ <u>The DNA test confirmed what Kay Rene had seen with her own eyes and what DeeAnn realized the second she met Kay Rene.</u> Kay Rene was not a Reed and had no **biological** link to her brother Bobby Reed. DeeAnn actually was Bobby Reed's sister and Kay Rene really was an Angell.

10 2-46

The news was shocking and disturbing for Kay Rene, who felt as if she had lived a lie. She questioned if ⓬ <u>her memories</u> actually belonged to her since she lived what should have been DeeAnn's life. DeeAnn finally got ⓭ <u>the answer</u> to why she had an affinity for horses. Her biological father had been a horse trainer. DeeAnn and Kay Rene have become close following the **revelation**. They refer to each other as ⓮ <u>swisters</u>, short for switched sisters.

11 2-47

The hospital where the women were born has offered them counseling, but neither has accepted the offer. "We're old women now," Kay Rene said. They also have not decided if they will **sue** the facility. And while DeeAnn harbors at least some anger about the situation, Kay Rene said she does not because there is no use in it.

NOTES　Washington「米国ワシントン州：西海岸の北部に位置する」　affinity「好み」　harbor「…を心に抱く」

⓫ DNA検査を受けた結果、どんなことがはっきりしたでしょうか。"The DNA test ..."で始まる文を訳しましょう。

訳：_____

⓬ Kay Reneが衝撃を受けて混乱した理由は何でしょうか。"her memories"とはどんなものかも考えながら、まとめてみましょう。

her memories：_____

理由：自分が＿＿＿＿＿＿を生きている。本来なら＿＿＿＿＿＿＿はずの人生を自分が生きているので、自分の＿＿＿＿＿が＿＿＿＿＿＿なのかと感じたため。

⓭ DeeAnnが得た答えとは、どのような疑問に対するものだったでしょうか。前のブロック（**7**と**8**）の内容も踏まえながら答えましょう。

UNIT 4 ETHICAL ISSUES

⓮ "swisters"とは造語ですが、これと同じ意味を表す語句を本文中から抜き出しましょう。また、適切な日本語の意味を考えてみましょう。

同じ語句：＿＿＿＿＿＿＿＿＿＿＿＿＿＿＿＿＿＿＿＿

意味：＿＿＿＿＿＿＿＿＿＿＿＿＿＿＿＿＿＿＿＿＿

⓯ 第3〜5ブロック（4〜6、7と8、9〜11）のそれぞれの内容にふさわしい見出しを下から選んで、[ ]に記入しましょう。

- Growing Up with Questions
- 'Swisters': Switched Sisters
- Switched at Birth: Uncovering the Truth

Information Organization

▶ 下の表を使って、本文の内容を整理しましょう。空欄にあてはまる語を英語で記入しましょう。空欄に入る語は1語とは限りません。

Question	Answer
What happened?	Two babies were (1.) and given to the (2.) mothers.
When did this happen?	In 1953.
Where did this happen?	At a (3.).
How did this happen?	Nurses switched the babies when (4.).
Who was Kay Rene's biological mother?	(5.).
Who was DeeAnn's biological mother?	Mrs. Reed.
How did they learn the truth?	An 86-year-old woman called (6.) and told him that the babies were (7.). She was a former (8.) of the Angell family and had also known Mrs. Reed.

How does Kay Rene feel about what happened?	She is (9.) because she feels it is (10.) to be angry.
How does DeeAnn feel about what happened?	She still (11.) toward the hospital.

Short Summary

▶ 空欄に適する単語を記入して、本文全体の要約文を完成させましょう。

Two babies were (1.   ) at birth at a hospital in Oregon in 1953. After the babies were (2.   ), the nurses gave the wrong babies to their mothers. DeeAnn was given to Mrs. Angell, and Kay Rene was given to Mrs. Reed. In the hospital, Mrs. Angell (3.   ) that she had been given the wrong baby, but no one would believe her. Many years later, an (4.   ) neighbor called Bobby Reed, Kay Rene's brother. She told him the truth about the switch. Soon after, Kay Rene and DeeAnn had (5.   ) which proved that they really had been switched at birth.

Critical Thinking

▶ 以下の質問について自分の意見をまとめましょう。そして、ペアやグループで話し合ったり、クラスで発表したりしましょう。

1. Kay Rene Reed Qualls said she enjoyed a wonderful life, but she still feels guilty. Why do you think she feels this way?

2. What do you think Kay Rene and DeeAnn will do in the future, now that they know the truth? Will they become close to their biological families? Will they become close to each other? Will they decide to sue the hospital?

CHAPTER 12

Saving Her Sister's Life

Pre-reading Preparation

▶ 次の語句の意味を確認しましょう。この章のテーマとも共通するキーワードの単語は何だと思いますか。タイトルも参考に考えてみましょう。

[bone marrow / cornea / heart / kidney / liver / lung / pancreas]

キーワード：＿＿＿＿＿＿＿＿＿＿＿＿＿＿

Vocabulary

▶ 下の語句の意味を調べ、表に記入しましょう。次に、英語の説明として適切なものを枠内から選び、記号で答えましょう。

語句	意味	説明
1. stir		
2. conceive		
3. diagnose		
4. donor		
5. practically		

語句	意味	説明
6. heritage		
7. stimulate		
8. critic		
9. solely		
10. personally		

a. someone who gives a part of their body to help a person who is ill
b. in person
c. a person who expresses an unfavorable opinion of something
d. all the qualities that have been passed on from one generation to another
e. to identify a particular illness or problem
f. not involving anyone or anything else
g. to arouse strong feeling in someone; to move or excite
h. virtually; almost but not completely or exactly
i. to become pregnant
j. to cause a part of the body to work or start working

Reading Analysis

▶ 英文を読んで、問いに答えましょう。

1 [2-48]

　*In 1990, Marissa Ayala's birth **stirred*** ❶ *a national debate—should families **conceive** one child to save another's life? In her own words, 18-year-old Marissa shares her story.*

2 [2-49]

　My sister, Anissa, is like my second mom. Even though she is 18 years older than me, I do not know how much closer you could be with someone. In 1988, when she was 16, Anissa was **diagnosed** with leukemia. If she did not find a bone marrow **donor**, doctors said, she would die within three to five years. My parents were not matches, so for a few years they went through every organization they could—the Life-Savers Foundation of America, the National Marrow Donor Program, City of Hope—to find donors. They could not find a single match. At the time, the Hispanic rating for the National Marrow Donor Program was **practically** nonexistent, which means there were hardly any Hispanics on the list as donors. ❸ Since that's our **heritage**, it was not likely my parents would find someone who could work as a match for my sister.

3 [2-50]

　Because matches are more common within families than with nonrelatives, every single extended family member got tested, but none of them matched with Anissa. Finally, one of my mom's best friends said as a joke, "Mary, you should have another baby." My mom, who was 43 at the time, thought her friend was crazy. But one night my mom dreamed that God was telling her to have a baby. She took that as a sign, and in April 1990 I was born. My parents were hoping I would be a match.

> **NOTES** leukemia「白血病」　bone marrow「骨髄」　Life-Savers Foundation of America「全米ライフセーバーズ基金」
> National Marrow Donor Program「全米骨髄バンク」
> City of Hope「シティ・オブ・ホープ：国立がん研究所が指定した総合がんセンター」　nonexistent「実在しない」
> nonrelative「親族でない者」

❶ "a national debate" の具体的な内容は何でしょうか。

_____

❷ 第2パラグラフを読んで、Anissa についてまとめましょう。

　　1988年、＿＿＿歳のときに白血病と診断され、＿＿＿＿＿＿＿をしなければ余命は＿＿＿＿年と言われた。両親はドナーとして適合しなかったためあらゆる手を尽くして探したが、Anissa に適合するドナーは＿＿＿＿＿＿＿＿＿＿＿＿。

❸ "Since ..." で始まる文の内容に合うように、次の文章の空欄を埋めましょう。

The Ayala family is (　　　　　　　). As there were few Hispanic donors on the list then, it seemed to be nearly (　　　　　　　) for the parents to find a (　　　　　) for Anissa.

❹ 母親がAnissaのためにもう一人子どもを産もうと思った最初のきっかけは何でしたか。また、彼女が決心するきっかけとなった出来事は何でしたか。

最初のきっかけ：_____

_____

決心するきっかけ：_____

4

When I was old enough to be tested, I turned out to be a perfect match for my sister. My family was really excited and had me donate bone marrow to her 14 months after I was born—my marrow was transplanted into hers to **stimulate** healthy blood-cell growth. It was a total success. I recovered perfectly—my parents even have a video of me running around the same day I had my surgery. Although at first my sister had to be in an isolation room for a while so that no germs could get to her, she recovered well. She has been cancer-free for the past 18 years.

5

There has always been a lot of ❼ media attention surrounding our family because of our situation, though. ❽ It was apparently really controversial that (_____). I do not remember a lot of that, because I was so much younger. When I was a baby, Anissa and I were on the cover of *Time* and there was a made-for-TV movie on NBC in 1993 called *For the Love of My Child: The Anissa Ayala Story*, made about my family's experience.

6

I first started really researching my own story when I was in the seventh grade. My friends were Googling themselves and nothing came up, but when I searched for myself a lot of news articles popped up. ❾ I read negative comments from a few newspapers about how my parents were just using me to save my sister's life and were not going to love me, and that what they did was morally wrong. It surprised me. I thought, "Really? People think about my family like that?" Some of the articles said that if I had not been a perfect match for my sister, my parents would have disowned me. And that just was not the case.

7

I try to see ❿ both sides of the story, but I ultimately do not agree with ⓫ the **critics**. They were probably just looking out for my safety, thinking that my parents were going to have a baby **solely** for the purpose of saving their child. But they do not know us **personally**: My family loves me so much.

NOTES　transplant「…を移植する」　blood-cell「血球」　germ「細菌」　morally「道徳的に」　disown「…を自分のものだと認めない」

❺ 移植の手術が行われたのはいつでしょうか。

　　_____年___月

❻ 移植手術の結果と二人の術後の経過はどうだったでしょうか。

　　手術の結果：_____

　　Marissa：_____

　　Anissa：_____

❼ "media attention" の具体例を2つ、英語で挙げましょう。

　　■ _____
　　■ _____

❽ この移植手術が、普通のケースと違ってメディアの注目を浴びた理由は何でしょうか。"It was apparently really controversial ..." で始まる文を完成させましょう。

　　It was apparently really controversial that (
　　　　　　　　　　　　　　　　　　　　　　　　　　　　　　　　　).

❾ "I read ..." で始まる文を訳しましょう。

　　_____
　　_____
　　_____

❿ "both sides" とは、具体的にどのような意味でしょうか。空欄を埋めて答えましょう。

　　both (　　　　　　　) and (　　　　　　　　) sides

⓫ "the critics" はどのような捉え方をしていたと Marissa は考えていましたか。

　　_____
　　_____

⓬ 最終的に Marissa が、彼女の家族を批判する人たちの考えには賛成できないと思った理由は何でしょうか。それを表している箇所に波下線（～～～）を引き、その内容を日本語で答えましょう。

　　内容：_____
　　_____

8

Every year our family takes part in the Relay for Life cancer walk and we raise money for the American Cancer Society. We try to spread ⓮ the message that the need for marrow donors is great. And more important, that despite being diagnosed with whatever type of cancer, there is a way to get through it.

9

There are so many ways growing up as ⓯ "the baby who saved her sister" has influenced my life. I have taken it, been humbled by it, and have grown from it. But it will not be my whole life story. In the future, I plan to study either child development or psychology. My dad always tells me, "Marissa, you should do something you want to do every day." I want to help people.

NOTES Relay for Life「リレー・フォー・ライフ：American Cancer Society が国際ライセンスを持っている企画で、がん患者や家族を支援するチャリティー活動」 American Cancer Society「アメリカ対がん協会」 humble「…を謙虚にする」

⓭ Ayala 家の人たちは、現在どのような活動をしていますか。

_____

_____

⓮ "the message" の具体的な内容は何でしょうか。

_____

_____

⓯ "the baby who saved her sister" であることが、Marissa の現在の人生にどのような影響を与えていますか。また、将来についてはどうですか。

現在：_____

将来：_____

Information Organization

▶ 下のフローチャートを使って、本文の内容を整理しましょう。空欄にあてはまる語を英語で記入しましょう。空欄に入る語は1語とは限りません。

Anissa Ayala was (1.　　　　　) with leukemia and needed a bone marrow transplant.

↓

Anissa's parents (2. 　　　　　) matches.
Anissa's parents checked lists looking for a bone marrow donor.
Because the Ayala family is Hispanic and few Hispanics were on the lists, finding a donor was very (3. 　　　　　).

↓

All their own relatives were (4. 　　　　　) as bone marrow donors.
Nobody was a good match.

↓

Anissa's parents decided to have (5. 　　　　　) who might be a donor.

↓

The baby, Marissa, was born.
Marissa was tested and was a good match to (6. 　　　　　) bone marrow to Anissa.
Bone marrow was taken from baby Marissa and given to Anissa.
Anissa (7. 　　　　　) and both girls have had normal lives for (8. 　　　　　).

↓

Marissa became a teenager and learned she had been (9. 　　　　　) as a baby.
Her parents' decision was widely reported in the (10. 　　　　　) and some people criticized them.
Marissa read all of the old media coverage and decides the (11. 　　　　　) had been wrong.

↓

The Ayala family continues to promote bone marrow donation.
Marissa thinks about her future and considers studying (12. 　　　　　) or psychology.

Short Summary

▶ 空欄に適する単語を記入して、本文全体の要約文を完成させましょう。

The Ayala family had a daughter, Anissa, with leukemia who needed a bone marrow (¹.   ). The best (².   ) are relatives. Many relatives were tested, but they were not good matches. The way the Ayalas filled their daughter's need was to have another child who could (³.   ) bone marrow to her older sister. The strategy might not have worked. However, the younger sister, Marissa, turned out to be a perfect bone marrow (⁴.   ). Many people criticized the Ayalas for having a child with a medical purpose. The younger Ayala sister, however, never thought anything was strange. She was happy to (⁵.   ) her older sister and also live a normal life.

Critical Thinking

▶ 以下の質問について自分の意見をまとめましょう。そして、ペアやグループで話し合ったり、クラスで発表したりしましょう。

1. What do you think is the general opinion on living to living organ donation in your country? Is this practice legal? How are the policies similar in various countries? How are they different?

2. What is your opinion about the Ayala case? Do you approve of their decision to have another child in order to save their daughter?

CHAPTER 1 The Birth-Order Myth

1 "No wonder he's so charming and funny—he's the baby of the family!" "She works hard trying to please the boss. I bet she's a firstborn." "Anyone that selfish has to be an only child."

2 It has long been part of folk wisdom that birth order strongly affects personality, intelligence, and achievement. However, most of the research claiming that firstborns are radically different from other children has been discredited, and it now seems that any effects of birth order on intelligence or personality will likely be washed out by all the other influences in a person's life. In fact, the belief in the permanent impact of birth order, according to Toni Falbo, a social psychologist at the University of Texas at Austin, "comes from the psychological theory that your personality is fixed by the time you're six. That assumption simply is incorrect."

3 The better, later, and larger studies are less likely to find birth order a useful predictor of anything. When two Swiss social scientists, Cecile Ernst and Jules Angst, reviewed 1,500 studies a few years ago, they concluded that "birth-order differences in personality ... are nonexistent in our sample. In particular, there is no evidence for a 'firstborn personality.'"

Putting Birth Order in Context

4 Of the early studies that seemed to show birth order mattered, most failed to recognize how other factors could confuse the issue. Take family size: Plenty of surveys showed that eldest children were overrepresented among high achievers. However, that really says less about being a firstborn than about not having many siblings, or any at all. After all, any group of firstborns is going to include a disproportionate number of children from small families, since every family has a firstborn but fewer have a fourthborn. Most experts now believe that position in the family means little when taken out of the context of *everything* going on in a particular household—whether sibling rivalry is **promoted** or **discouraged**, for instance.

5 Parents who believe that firstborns are more **capable** or **deserving** may treat them differently, thus setting up a self-fulfilling prophecy.

Old Theories Die Hard

6 Consider the question of whether birth order affects achievement or intelligence. Many experts today suggest that birth order plays no role at all. When Judith Blake, a demographer at the University of California, Los Angeles, looked at birth patterns before 1938 and compared them to SAT scores for that group of children, she found no connection. On the other hand, the *number* of siblings does matter. "Small families are, on average, much more **supportive** of the kind of **verbal** ability that helps people succeed in school," Blake says. The reason, she believes, is that parental attention is diluted in larger families.

7 As for effects on personality, results are mixed. Research suggests that you are somewhat more likely to be outgoing, well-adjusted and independent if you grew up with few or no siblings. Two recent studies, however, found no differences on the basis of size alone. The only **certainty** is that there do not seem to be any *disadvantages* to growing up in a small family—

including being an only child. After reviewing 141 studies, Falbo and a colleague found that being raised with or without siblings does not affect personality in predictable ways. Where small differences were found—such as in achievement **motivation**—they favored the only children.

Do Kids Need More Space?

8   If position does not control destiny and family size has only a minor impact, what about spacing between children? Although little research has been conducted, some psychologists believe there are more advantages to having kids far apart rather than close together. Some specialists caution that siblings close in age may be treated as a single unit.

9   This is eyebrow-raising news, given that parents are sometimes advised not to wait too long before having a second child. However, different studies have led to different conclusions. One found that a firstborn was more likely to have high **self-esteem** if his or her sibling was *less* than two years younger. Another indicated that spacing had no impact on social **competence**, and others note positive effects for boys but not for girls.

10 As with birth order, cautions about jumping to conclusions may be ignored by the general public. As Blake says: "You're never going to completely put to rest what people think is fun to believe."

(718 words)

CHAPTER 2   My Husband, the Outsider

1 When my husband-to-be and I announced our engagement, people were curious about the kind of wedding we would have. He is an Irish-Ukrainian from the Bronx, and a lapsed Catholic, while I am an American-born Korean from New Jersey. Some of my husband's friends must have been expecting an exotic wedding ceremony.

2 We disappointed many people. Far from being exotic, or even very **religious**, our ceremony was performed in English by a Unitarian minister on a hotel balcony. But when my husband and I decided to have 50 guests instead of 150, we caused an uproar among **relatives** and family friends, especially on the Korean side.

3 "It's very embarrassing," my father complained. "Everyone wants to know why you won't listen to me and invite the people you should."

"Well, whose wedding is this, anyway?" I asked.

4 What a dumb question. I had forgotten for a moment that I was dealing with Koreans. It was bad enough that I had decided to marry a non-Korean, but highly **insulting** that I was not giving everyone the chance to snicker over it in person. I found out after the wedding that my father was asked, "How does it feel to have an American son-in-law?"

"My son-in-law is a good man," he said. "Better to have a good American son-in-law than a bad Korean one."

5 He had not always felt that way. For years, he ignored the non-Koreans I was dating—it took him about a year to remember my husband's name. But when I was a freshman in college, I dated my father's dream of a son-in-law, David, an American-born Korean from a respected family, who was doing brilliantly at Harvard and had plans for law school. When the relationship ended, my father preferred not to **acknowledge** the fact.

6 When it became clear that David would never be his son-in-law, my father started dropping hints at the dinner table about some handsome and **delightful** young doctor working for him, who was right off the plane from Seoul—there seemed to be a steady supply. This started during my senior year in college, and continued until sometime after my engagement.

7 The one time I did go out with a Korean doctor was at my mother's request. "Please, just once," she said. "One of my college friends has a son who wants to get married, and she thought of you."

"You expect me to go out with a guy who lets his mommy pick his dates?" I asked.

"He's very traditional," she explained. "If you refuse to meet him, my friend will think I'm too snobby to want her son in our family. I'll lose face."

8 "OK, just this once," I said **reluctantly**. A few days later, I sat in an Indian restaurant with the Korean doctor. After several start-and-stop attempts at conversation, the doctor told me I should live in Korea for a while.

9 "Korea is a great country," he said. "I think you ought to **appreciate** it more. And you should learn to speak Korean. I don't understand why you can't speak your native language."

"English is my native language," I said. "I wish I could speak Korean, but I don't have the time to learn it now."

"You are Korean," he insisted. "You should speak your mother tongue." A mouthful of food kept me from saying more than "Mmmm," but I found myself stabbing my tandoori chicken with remarkable violence.

10 Despite our obvious incompatibility, the doctor kept asking me out. For weeks, I had to turn down invitations to dinner, movies and concerts—even rides to visit my parents—before he finally stopped calling.

11 During a visit to Seoul a few years later, I realized that this kind of dogged **persistence** during Korean courtship was quite common. In fact, my own father had used it successfully. My mother told me he proposed to her the day after they were introduced at a dinner given by matchmaking friends. She told him he was crazy when she turned him down. Undaunted, he hounded her for three months until she finally gave in.

12 My parents have now been married for almost 40 years, but what worked for them was not about to work for me. I think one reason my father did not object to having a non-Korean son-in-law—aside from actually liking my husband—was that he was relieved to have one at all.

When I was 24, he started asking me, "When are you going to make me a grandfather?"

13 And when I turned 25, the age when unmarried women in Korea are considered old maids, my other relatives expressed their concern.

"You better hurry up and meet someone," one of my aunts told me. "Do you have a boyfriend?"

"Yes," I said …. I had met my future husband a few months earlier in an office where I was working as a temporary secretary.

"Is he Korean?" she asked.

"No." My aunt considered this for a moment, then said, "You better hurry up and meet someone. Do you want me to help?"

14 My husband saved me from spinsterhood. Just barely, in some eyes—I was married at 26. We received **generous** gifts, many from people who had not been invited to the wedding. This convinced my father more than ever that we should have invited all of his friends and relatives. He felt this way for several years, until one of my sisters got engaged and made **elaborate** plans to feed and entertain 125 wedding guests.

15 As the expenses mounted, my father took me aside and asked me to talk to my sister.

"Tell her she should have a small simple wedding," he said. "Like yours."

(944 words)

CHAPTER 3 Hop, Skip … and Software?

1. Jody Spanglet's seventh- and eighth-grade students at Charlottesville Waldorf School in Virginia are studying revolutions. They dissect the Declaration of Independence, delve into the French rebellion against Louis XIV, and read about the various inventors who sparked the Industrial Revolution. But this study happens to be profoundly counterrevolutionary in today's cyber age: Not a single classroom in the school—from kindergarten through eighth grade—contains a computer.

2. Contrast that with the B.F. Yancey Elementary School in the southwest corner of the same county, Albemarle, in central Virginia. Here, computers are considered a rich resource and are used everywhere, from kindergarten through fifth grade. Third graders working on oral history projects, for example, must first pass an online minicourse. They can then take home digital video cameras and download their oral history interviews onto the school computers, which are later made available on the school's website.

3. While the computerless Waldorf School is an **exception** in a nation that tends to **embrace** the technology revolution, both schools find themselves on the cutting edge of a debate about if and how computers should be introduced to children at the elementary school level. At one end of the spectrum are coalitions such as the Alliance for Childhood, which has called for a moratorium on computers for students in early childhood and elementary schools. Concerns range from health issues to the need for stronger bonds between children and adults and more hands-on, active play in learning. At the other end are educators and technology **enthusiasts**, who believe that the use of computers at an early age—even when led by an adult—can open a child's mind to ideas and concepts that will kindle a great desire for learning, and perhaps make a child "smarter." Parents and guardians stand somewhere in the middle.

4. Many parents, who brag that their not-yet-three-year-old can type his or her name on a keyboard to enter a computer game, also admit to a grudging guilt that they did not instead send that same toddler outdoors to explore the wonders of blooming crocuses peeking through a layer of snow. "I don't think an elementary school **virtually** devoid of technology is necessarily bad," says Gene Maeroff, a professor at Columbia University's Teachers College and the author of "A Classroom of One: How Online Learning Is Changing Our Schools and Colleges." "Nor do I think a school loaded with technology is necessarily good, or better, at meeting students' needs," he says. "Computers can enhance education. But those possibilities become greater as kids get older, particularly at the secondary level and absolutely at the college or postgraduate level."

5. Various studies show different effects of computer use in the classroom. In the late 1990s, the Educational Testing Service found that middle school students with well-trained teachers who used computers for "simulations and applications" in math class **outperformed** students on standardized tests who had not used them for that purpose. Meanwhile, eighth graders whose teachers used computers primarily for "drill and practice" performed even worse.

Born Digital

[6] Computer technology is a fact of life in U.S. schools and homes. Currently, 98 percent of public schools have access to the Internet in their schools. And one in five students in public schools overall have access to a computer. In urban schools, that number drops to one in nine—which one technology advocate calls "not a digital divide, but a digital chasm." Today, according to the National Center for Educational Statistics, 80 percent of eighth graders have access to a computer at home. Despite tightened state budgets, efforts are under way throughout the country to make technology even more **relevant to** students and learning. In Maine, every single seventh grader (of whom there are slightly more than 18,000) has a laptop computer. In April, the state will begin sending computers to all eighth graders, too. At Walton Middle School in Charlottesville, Virginia, seventh graders are using what some predict will be the educational technology of the future—handheld computers—to **facilitate** writing.

[7] But how computers are used varies greatly. Elliot Soloway, of the University of Michigan's Center for Highly Interactive Computing in Education, surveyed 4,000 schools last year and found that 65 percent of students in public schools, including high schools, spend less than 15 minutes a week using computers to access the Internet. *PC Magazine* reports that, of the $5 billion spent in the past decade to get computers into schools, 17 percent was used to educate teachers how to use the computers and **integrate** them into the curriculum. That gets to the heart of a debate over whether computer use in school is beneficial to students—or merely expensive window dressing.

[8] Quality teachers have always worked toward finding many different paths to build basic knowledge and skills that students will need to succeed in school and life, says Becky Fisher, assistant director of the Department of Technology for the Albemarle County Schools. "Adding technology to the mix only makes a great teacher even better," she says. "The issue is not whether technology is appropriate for students—most kindergartners have already mastered more technology than existed when I was a child. Rather, it is whether our teachers are supported in a way to maximize the benefits of technology."

The Human Connection

[9] Those who think technology in the classroom should wait see technology differently. "We strongly believe that actual experience is **vital** for young children," says Jody Spanglet of the Waldorf School in Charlottesville. "It is important for students to interact with one another, with teachers, and with the world—to explore ideas, participate in the creative process, and develop their knowledge, skills, abilities, and inner qualities." Nancy Regan, an administrator at the school, says: "A computer is a mediated experience. You touch the keyboard, but what happens online is not your doing. Our whole curriculum is based on human connection."

[10] It is not that the Waldorf School eschews technology. For example, it has a website. And Ms. Regan says computers at the high school level are a good idea. Her seventh and eighth graders will soon be doing a report on inventors from the Industrial Revolution. To do so, they

are required to use at least three resources, one of which can be the Internet. Kim McCormick, who has two daughters, ages five and eight, at the Charlottesville Waldorf School says her family is not the least bit uncomfortable that their children's classrooms have no instructional computers. "We want them to get to know the world on a firsthand basis," says Ms. McCormick, a public school teacher. Her husband is a computer program analyst. "They see us using computers for work. But we don't have any kids' things on our computer. I have looked up butterflies for them before, so they know it can be a tool and resource. But they will learn to use a computer so quickly later. My husband, who works with computers for a living, didn't learn those skills until after college."

Going Online, Bit By Bit

11 Technology enthusiasts say computers should be introduced in stages. Paula White is a resource teacher for gifted students who helps integrate technology into the classroom at Yancey. White says that, at Yancey, while even kindergartners are using computers in the classroom—to count candy hearts on Valentine's Day, for instance—the teacher is the one entering the information. It is not as though children at Yancey are being plunked in front of a machine without interacting with teachers. But at some schools, lack of interaction is a real concern. A mother of three children in another Virginia elementary school says she is disappointed in the use of computers in two of her children's classes. When they get computer time, it is usually in the morning or late afternoon, she says, when a teacher wants to grab some extra time at his or her desk.

12 Bette Manchester of the Maine Learning Technology Initiative, which **oversees** the state's laptop project, says even the best teachers have a hard time incorporating the four or five desk computers that often sit in elementary classrooms. One-to-one computer access changes everything. "We've made this crystal clear: This is not about technology or software, it is about teaching kids," Ms. Manchester says. The success of the Maine program, she notes, depends heavily on leadership among teachers in the state, as well as the complete integration of laptops into every school's curriculum. Training involves teachers, staff, students, and parents, and started well before the computers arrived. Manchester says middle school is a great time to give students intimate access to the technology. "They are at a critical stage developmentally," she says. "These kids are learning how to learn, not simply reading to learn anymore. It's been very exciting watching them take off."

(1,453 words)

CHAPTER 4 Highs and Lows in Self-Esteem

[1] No one in the Gould family of Westlake Village, California, was surprised by a study suggesting a person's age and stage of life may have a bigger impact on self-esteem than we ever realized. A study of about 350,000 people likens a person's self-esteem across the human lifespan to a roller coaster ride, starting with an inflated sense of self-approval in late childhood that **plunges** in adolescence. Self-esteem rises steadily through adulthood, only to drop to its lowest point ever in old age. "I've gone through pretty much all of those cycles," Fred Gould said. At 60, he is edging toward retirement. Fred's wife, Eileen, 46, is a businesswoman in the throes of mid-adulthood and, according to the study, predisposed to a healthy self-regard. At 21, the Goulds' son, Jeff, has just **launched** that heady climb into adulthood and a buoyant self-regard after an adolescence fraught with the usual perils of self-doubt and hormonal warfare. His sister, Aly, 17, disagrees with a lot of the study, believing instead that each individual has an intrinsic sense of self-esteem that remains relatively constant. But she does agree that adolescence can give even the most solid sense of self-esteem a sound battering. "As a teenager, I can definitely speak for all of us when I say we bag on ourselves," Aly said.

The Study

[2] The drop in self-esteem in adolescence was no surprise to Richard Robins, a psychology professor at the University of California at Davis, who spearheaded the study, but "the drop in old age is a little bit more novel," he said. Specifically, Robins was intrigued by the **similarities** in self-esteem levels between those entering adolescence and old age. "There is an accumulation of losses occurring all at once both in old age and adolescence," he suggested. "There is a critical mass of **transition** going on."

[3] Those answering the survey ranged in age from 9 to 90. They participated in the survey by logging onto a Web site during a period between 1999 and 2000. About three-quarters were Caucasian, the rest a mixture of people of Asian, black, Latino and Middle-Eastern descent. Most were from the United States. The survey simply asked people to agree or strongly disagree—on a five-point scale—with the statement: "I see myself as someone who has high self-esteem."

[4] Everybody is an individual, Robins stressed, so self-esteem can be affected by a number of things that are biological, social, and situational, but there are certain passages that all of us face—and each passage can have a powerful effect on our sense of self. "With kids, their feelings about themselves are often based on relatively superficial information," Robins explained. "As we get older, we base our self-esteem on actual achievements and **feedback** from other people."

[5] **Overall**, the study indicated that women do not fare as well as men in self-esteem—a difference particularly marked in adolescence. "During adolescence, girls' self-esteem dropped about twice as much as boys'," Robins said, perhaps at least partially because of society's heavy emphasis on body image for girls. Add one negative life event to all of this turmoil, and a teenager's delicate self-esteem can crumble.

Emerging into Adulthood

6   Eileen remembered having fairly high self-esteem from ages 12 to 16. She had been very ill as a child, so the teen years were a time for her to blossom. Then, her mother died when she was 17, and her self-esteem bottomed out. "I was like, 'What do I do? How do I handle this?'" Eileen remembered. Eileen was 22 when she married Fred, an event that **coincided** with the beginning of her adult years—and an upswing in her self-esteem. Like many adults, Eileen gained her senses of competence and **continuity**, both of which can contribute to the rise in self-esteem during the adult years, Robins said.

7   Even if there is divorce or some other form of **chaos**, there has been a change in our ability to cope, he said. We learn with experience. Fred is aware that his sense of self-esteem may be **vulnerable** when he retires. "I'm concerned about keeping my awareness level," he said. "Am I going to be aware of the social scene? Of things more global? Am I going to be able to read and keep up with everything?"

8   Seniors do tend to experience a drop in self-esteem when they get into their 70s, the study says—but not always. This is enigmatic to Robins. "When we look at things like general well-being, the evidence is mixed about what happens in old age," he said.

9   Some people experience a tremendous loss of self-esteem, whereas others maintain their sense of well-being right through old age. Others are not as lucky. Whereas adolescents lose their sense of childhood omnipotence, seniors experience another kind of loss. Retirement comes at about the same time seniors may begin to lose loved ones, their health, their financial status, or their sense of competence. Suddenly, someone who was so in charge may become withdrawn, sullen, and depressed. Their self-esteem may plummet. Robins hopes the study will make us more aware of the times when our self-esteem can be in jeopardy.   (856 words)

CHAPTER 5 Who Lives Longer?

[1] How to live longer is a topic that has fascinated mankind for centuries. Today, scientists are beginning to separate the facts from the fallacies surrounding the aging process. Why is it that some people reach a ripe old age and others do not? Several factors influencing **longevity** are set at birth, but surprisingly, many others are elements that can be changed. Here is what you should know.

[2] Some researchers divide the elements determining who will live longer into two categories: fixed factors and changeable factors. Gender, race and heredity are fixed factors—they cannot be reversed, although certain long-term social changes can influence them. For example, women live longer than men—at birth, their life expectancy is about seven to eight years more. However, cigarette smoking, drinking and reckless driving could shorten this advantage.

[3] There is increasing evidence that length of life is also influenced by a number of elements that are within your ability to control. The most obvious are physical lifestyle factors.

Health Measures

[4] According to a **landmark** study of nearly 7,000 adults in Alameda County, California, women can add up to seven years to their lives and men 11 to 12 years by following seven simple health practices: (1) Do not smoke. (2) If you drink, do so only moderately. (3) Eat breakfast regularly. (4) Do not eat between meals. (5) Maintain normal weight. (6) Sleep about eight hours a night. (7) Exercise moderately.

[5] Cutting calories may be the single most significant lifestyle change you can make. Experiments have shown that in laboratory animals, a 40 percent calorie reduction leads to a 50 percent extension in longevity. "Eating less has a more **profound** and diversified effect on the aging process than does any other life-style change," says Byung P. Yu, Ph.D., professor of physiology at the University of Texas Health Science Center at San Antonio. "It is the only factor we know of in laboratory animals that is an anti-aging factor."

Psychosocial Factors

[6] A long life, however, is not just the result of being good to your body and staving off disease. All the various factors that constitute and influence daily life can be critical too. In searching for the ingredients to a long, healthy existence, scientists are studying links between longevity and the psychological and social aspects of human existence. The following can play significant roles in determining your longevity:

Social Integration

[7] Researchers have found that people who are socially integrated—they are part of a family network, are married, participate in structured group activities—live longer.

[8] Early studies indicated that the more friends and relatives you had, the longer you lived. Newer studies focus on the types of relationships that are most **beneficial**. "Larger networks

don't always seem to be advantageous to women," says epidemiologist Teresa Seeman, Ph.D., associate research scientist at Yale University. "Certain kinds of ties add more demands rather than generate more help."

Autonomy

9   A feeling of **autonomy** or control can come from having a say in important decisions (where you live, how you spend your money) or from being surrounded by people who inspire confidence in your ability to master certain tasks (yes, you can quit smoking, you will get well). Studies show these feelings bring a sense of well-being and **satisfaction** with life. "Autonomy is a key factor in successful aging," says Toni Antonucci, associate research scientist at the Institute for Social Research at the University of Michigan.

Stress and Job Satisfaction

10   Researchers disagree on how these factors affect longevity. There is not enough data available to support a link between stress and longevity, says Edward L. Schneider, M.D., dean of the Andrus Gerontology Center at the University of Southern California. Animal research, however, provides exciting insights. In studies with laboratory rats, certain types of stress damage the **immune** system and destroy brain cells, especially those involved in memory. Other kinds of stress enhance immune function by 20 to 30 percent, supporting a theory first advanced by Hans Selye, M.D., Ph.D., a pioneer in stress research. He proposed that an exciting, active and meaningful life contributes to good health.

11   The relationship between job satisfaction and longevity also remains in question. According to some researchers, a satisfying job adds years to a man's life, while volunteer work increases a woman's longevity. These findings may change as more women participate in the workforce. One study found that clerical workers suffered twice as many heart attacks as homemakers. Factors associated with the coronary problems were **suppressed** hostility, having a nonsupportive boss, and decreased job mobility.

Environment

12   Where you live can make a difference in how long you live. A study by the California Department of Health Services in Berkeley found a 40 percent higher mortality rate among people living in a poverty area compared to those in a nonpoverty area. "The difference was not due to age, sex, health care or lifestyle," says George A. Kaplan, Ph.D., chief of the department's Human Population Laboratory. The resulting **hypothesis**: A locale can have environmental characteristics, such as polluted air or water, or socioeconomic characteristics, such as a high crime rate and level of stress, that make it unhealthy.

Socioeconomic Status

[13] People with higher incomes, more education and high-status occupations tend to live longer. Researchers used to think this was due to better living and job conditions, nutrition and access to health care, but these theories have not held up. Nevertheless, the differences can be dramatic. Among women 65 to 74 years old, those with less than an eighth-grade education are much more likely to die than are women who have completed at least one year of college.

What Can You Do?

[14] The message from the experts is clear. There are many ways to add years to your life. Instituting sound health practices and expanding your circle of **acquaintances** and activities will have a beneficial effect. The good news about aging, observes Erdman B. Palmore of the Center for the Study of Aging and Human Development at Duke Medical Center in North Carolina, is many of the factors related to longevity are also related to life satisfaction. (1,011 words)

CHAPTER 6 Are Gifted Children Born or Made?

1
Some say given enough time, money and instruction, any child can develop a special **expertise**. Others, however, insist gifted children are born, not made.

A Rage to Master

2
Gaven Largent, 13, has been playing music for five years. He started with guitar lessons at age eight, but not long after, he **quit**—not making music, just taking lessons. "I was not learning anything," he says. "I was just playing those notes on the paper; it was boring."

3
"Gaven became frustrated that it was sheet music and he was only playing the notes on the music," his mother Melissa says. "He wanted to fill it in and make it more." She says they knew when he was nine or ten that music would be his focus. "It became an **obsession** for him to figure out the sounds that he heard on a CD or the radio or live music."

4
That obsession is one of the trademarks of a gifted child, or prodigy, according to developmental psychologist Ellen Winner, who teaches at Boston College. "I say they have a **rage** to master. It is difficult to tear them away from the area in which they have high ability."

Looking Back as Former Child Prodigies

5
Julian Lage, who is now 21, remembers playing guitar for hours as a child. "You wake up and you eat and you play music and you sleep." Lage, who recently released his first CD, *Sounding Point*, started playing guitar at five. A few years later, he was the subject of a documentary film, *Jules at Eight*. Still, the title "child prodigy" was something he never felt he could relate to. "Younger musicians, my **contemporaries** who have been called child prodigies, they feel slighted because it does **undermine** the work ethic, the thousands of hours you put in just to be able to produce a sound on your instrument."

6
That is a sentiment echoed by Rasta Thomas, 27, who was also labeled a prodigy. He made dance history as a teenager, winning the Gold Medal in the Senior Men's Division of the **prestigious** Jackson International Ballet Competition in Jackson, Mississippi at the age of 14. He now headlines his own dance company, Bad Boys of Dance. "I think if you give any seven-year-old the training I had, you will get a product that is at the top of its game," Thomas says. "I have had hours and hours and a million dollars **invested** into the training that I received."

Enabling Talent to Flower

7
But Winner, the author of *Gifted Children: Myths and Realities*, disagrees. "You can't make a gifted child out of any child." Winner says prodigies are born with natural talent, but she does believe they "need to be enabled in order to have their ability flower." Both Julian Lage, who played with vibraphonist, Gary Burton at age 12, and Rasta Thomas, who studied at the Kirov Ballet Academy in Washington, say they had that support. But the success that both Lage and Thomas enjoy today as adults is **due to** much more. Winner says studies have shown that most music prodigies are unheard of as adults. "The gift of being a child prodigy is very different from the gift of being an adult creator," she says. "To be an adult creator means you have to

do something new, which means taking a risk." Both Lage and Thomas took that creative risk early, **composing** and choreographing while they were still in their teens. Gaven Largent is headed in that direction as well. "I do write," he says. "I have not written too many songs with lyrics, but that's something I'd like to work on." Right now, he adds, he is working on a gospel song.

(617 words)

CHAPTER 7   Students Dig into Sustainable Farming at Vermont College

[1] Devin Lyons typically starts his days this summer cooking breakfast with fresh eggs from the farm's chicken coop. Then, depending on the weather, he and a dozen other college students might cut hay in the field using a team of oxen, turn compost, or weed vegetable beds.

[2] While other college students are in stuffy classrooms, about a dozen are earning credit tending a Vermont farm. For 13 weeks, 12 credits and about $12,500, the Green Mountain College students **plow** fields with oxen or horses, milk cows, weed crops, and grow and make their own food, part of an **intensive** course in **sustainable agriculture** using the least amount of fossil fuels. "Lots of schools study sustainable agriculture, but I don't think any of them put it into practice," said spokesman Kevin Coburn.

[3] There are no tractors on the 22 acres next to the brick campus of the small liberal arts college on the edge of the town—just two teams of oxen, and goats, pigs, two cows, and chickens. Students sleep in tents on the field's edge, next to a river. They spend about six hours a week in classes in the old farmhouse, learning theory on **organic** crop and animal management, management of farm systems, development of agricultural technologies with a focus on human and animal power, and the social and cultural importance of **regional** food. The rest of the time they are out in the field, or doing homework and working on research projects. "So they're actually seeing the **applications** firsthand," said Kenneth Mulder, manager of the college's Cerridwen Farm, who runs the summer program.

[4] College farming is growing. According to the Rodale Institute in Pennsylvania, more than 80 schools now have hands-on and classroom-based farm programs. Many of them are organic vegetable farms, but students do not necessarily earn as many credits as Green Mountain College students do, nor do they get to work with teams of oxen. Sterling College, also in Vermont, has a similar program. "It's traditionally been one of the leaders in environmental studies and it is because they put their studies where their mouth is in really getting students out and doing and practicing the sort of environmentally **enlightened** work that some talk about in class," said Roland King, a spokesman for the National Association of Independent Colleges and Universities.

[5] For her research project, Cassie Callahan, 18, Conway, N.H., wants to water plants with gray water collected from the farm's solar shower, attached to the greenhouse. But she is not sure yet if the soap—even biodegradable soap—will harm the plants if it is not diluted. Her real love is working with **draft** horses. She jumps at the chance every time and even has a new tattoo of a team of horses on her shin. In her hometown, she had a job driving horse-drawn sleighs and wagons and now has learned the animals can be used for more than tourism. She hopes to be a farmer, supporting herself and selling a little on the side. "You know, people have jobs to make money to feed themselves and clothe themselves but I'd much rather have my job be to feed and clothe myself," she said.

[6] Green Mountain College hopes to turn out farmers and has several alumni running farms nearby. Other students are interested in food-related fields—whether it is organizing nonprofits, working on policy or overseas development work. Lyons, 19, does not know if he will

farm but so far he has learned a lot. Growing up in **suburban** Jefferson, N.J., he said he did not know much about where his food came from and was never exposed to organic farms. "I never really got the connection between the cooked chicken on my plate—and it was a dead chicken that was killed—I just never really thought about it," he said.

(639 words)

CHAPTER 8 Wilder Places for Wild Things

 1 The beavers at the Minnesota Zoo seem engaged in an unending task. Each week they fell scores of inch-thick young trees for their winter food supply. Each week zoo workers surreptitiously replace the downed trees, anchoring new ones in the iron holders so the animals can keep on cutting. Letting the beavers do what comes naturally has paid off: Minnesota is one of the few zoos to get them to **reproduce** in captivity. The chimps at the St. Louis Zoo also work for a living: they poke stiff pieces of hay into an anthill to scoop out the baby food and honey that curators hide inside. Instead of idly awaiting banana handouts, the chimps get to manipulate tools, just as they do in the wild. Last year, when 13 gorillas moved into Zoo Atlanta's new $4.5 million rain forest, they mated and formed families—a rarity among captives. "Zoos have changed from being mere menageries to being celebrations of life," says John Gwynne of the Bronx Zoo. "As the wild places get smaller, the role of zoos gets larger, which means intensifying the naturalness of the experience for both visitors and animals."

 2 Naturalistic zoos are hardly new: animals liberated from concrete cages have been romping on Bronx savannas since 1941. But as species become extinct at a rate unparalleled since the Cretaceous era and 100 acres of tropical forests vanish every minute, zoos are **striving** to make their settings match their new role as keepers of the biological flame. Since 1980 the nation's 143 accredited zoos and aquariums have spent more than $1 billion on renovation and construction, much of it going to create **habitats** that immerse both animals and visitors in the sights, sounds, feel and smell of the wild. Today's best exhibits reproduce not just the look but also the function of a natural habitat: they encourage the residents to mate, to raise young and to develop the survival skills they would need on the savannas of Africa or the slopes of the Andes ....

 3 Lately, curators have been making exhibits not only look real but sound real. At the Bronx Zoo's lush Jungle World the shrieks of gibbons, the cacophony of crickets and the trills of hornbills emanate from 65 speakers. The zoo's resident audio expert, Tom Veltre, spent a month in Thailand stringing microphones and a mile of cables up and down mountains to capture the sounds of the jungle. Even though the animals figure out that the hoots and howls are coming from black boxes, and not from furry or feathered neighbors, the call of the wild can shape their behavior. At Healesville Sanctuary, outside Melbourne, Australia, nighttime sounds cue nocturnal platypuses when to sleep, says bio-acoustician Leslie Gilbert; realistic noises also snap gorillas out of stress-**induced** lethargy.

 4 "Natural" is now going beyond sight and sound to include everything from weather to activity patterns. Every day 11 rainstorms hit Tropic World at the Brookfield Zoo outside Chicago, **prompting** the monkeys to drop from their vines and scamper for cover amid cliffs, 50-foot-high gunite trees and 6,000 tropical plants. Regardless of the climate, the monkeys exhibit an array of behaviors never displayed in cages, such as rustling bushes to define their territories. At the San Diego Zoo's Sun Bear Forest, lion-tailed macaques are surrounded by jungle vines and cascading waterfalls. As soon as these highly endangered monkeys moved in last month, they fanned out and began foraging for fruit and other dainties left by the curators.

They even respond to the dominant male's alarm call by clustering around him—something keepers had never seen. At Seattle's Woodland Park Zoo, elephants in the exhibit that opened last month roll and stack logs just as they do in a Thai logging camp. The task relieves the pachyderms' boredom.

[5] Curators of rare species are focusing on how to induce one particular natural behavior—reproduction. At New York's Central Park Zoo, which reopened last year after a multimillion-dollar overhaul, the lights in the penguin house mimic seasonal changes in the austral day and night, which serve as a **crucial** cue for the birds' breeding cycle. At the San Diego Wild Animal Park, people are **confined** to cages (an electric monorail), and 2,600 animals roam free on 700 acres of veld and savanna. A white rhino that had never mated during 10 years at the San Diego Zoo has sired 55 offspring since moving into a 110-acre area at the park 17 years ago. "The difference is that he has room to mark out his territory and a harem [of 20] from which to choose," says spokesman Tom Hanscom. Getting flamingos to breed was simply a matter of providing more neighbors. For reasons curators cannot explain, the leggy pink birds never bred when they lived in two flocks of 50. But when merged into a group of 100 they began to build little mud mounds in the lake shallows on which to lay their eggs.

[6] Once fiercely competitive, most American zoos now participate in species-survival programs, intricate dating games for animals living far apart. Coordinated by the American Association of Zoological Parks and Aquariums, the SSP's rely on studbooks that keep track of zoo animals' age and ancestry, helping curators determine how to pair up males and females from member zoos to maintain the species' health and avoid inbreeding. Animals move back and forth between zoos to **ensure** the best genetic mix. Right now Indian rhinos from the Oklahoma City and National zoos are cozying up to the Bronx Zoo's female.

[7] Without such programs, many species would be extinct. "Zoos are becoming the last hope for a number of endangered species," says Ronald Tilson of the Minnesota Zoo. Indeed, there are more Siberian tigers in America's zoos than on Russia's northern tundra. For all their breeding successes, though, zoos will become little more than Noah's arks if nature continues to give way to pavement. That is why the new naturalistic settings are designed with people in mind, too. "Part of a zoo's reason for being is to inform the public of the marvelous things that occur on this planet," says Warren Thomas, director of the Los Angeles Zoo. "You do that by re-creating the environment that shaped these animals." In zoo parlance, it is called habitat immersion: getting visitors curious and excited about wild places and teaching them that habitat loss is the single greatest threat to wild animals today.

[8] In the rare cases when animals bred in captivity do have an ancestral home to return to, zoos are trying to **oblige** them. "The closer you come to mimicking nature in captivity, the easier that is," says primate curator Ann Baker of Brookfield. Already the Bronx Zoo has returned condors to the Andes. Scientists at the National Zoo in Washington taught a group of golden lion tamarins survival skills, such as how to forage and to heed warning calls, and have released 67 into a reserve near Rio de Janeiro since 1984. Although 35 died, others not

only survived but mated; so far, the freed animals have produced 13 surviving offspring. The San Diego Park has returned 49 oryxes—rare antelopes—to Oman, Jordan and Israel, where the graceful creatures have bred successfully. Black-foot ferrets, which a few years ago had dwindled to only 17 in the wild, have proliferated to 125 in captivity, and scientists plan to release the animals into prairie-dog territories in the Great Plains in a few years.

With every animal that moves onto the endangered species list, or drops off it by extinction, zoos assume greater importance. About 120 million people will visit U.S. zoos this year, giving curators 120 million chances to spread the conservation gospel. By showing how animals are shaped and supported by their environment, "zoos are trying to protect wild places as well as wild things," says Zoo Atlanta director Terry Maple. For as the wild places go, so go the wild animals.

(1,320 words)

CHAPTER 9 Antarctica: Whose Continent Is It Anyway?

[1] Last February, the World Discoverer, our cruise ship, stopped in front of a white ice cliff higher than the ship's mast. As large as France, the Ross Ice Shelf of Antarctica extends unbroken along the Ross Sea for hundreds of miles.

[2] Like other passengers on our cruise ship, we had been lured by an irresistible attraction: the chance to visit the most **remote** place on Earth, and the most unusual. The coldest place on Earth is also the subject of conflicting interests: scientists, tourists, environmentalists, oil and mineral seekers.

[3] Scientists **treasure** the unparalleled advantages for research; tourists prize the chance to visit Earth's last frontier; environmentalists fear that increases in both activities will pollute the continent and jeopardize its fabulous creatures; others contend that preserving Antarctica as a kind of world park will **deprive** the rest of the world of much needed oil and mineral reserves.

[4] Fears of Antarctica's **ruin** through commercial exploitation have been partly reduced by the October, 1991, 31-nation signing of the Madrid Protocol, which bans oil and gas exploration for the next 50 years. But Antarctica's unique attributes—it is the coldest, driest, and highest continent—will keep it at the focus of conflicting scientific and touristic interests.

[5] Think of a place as remote as the far side of the moon, as strange as Saturn and as inhospitable as Mars, and that will give some idea of what Antarctica is like. A mere 2.4 percent of its 5.4 million-square-mile land mass is ice-free, and then, only for a few months a year. Scientists estimate that 70 percent of the world's fresh water is locked away in Antarctica's icecap; if it were ever to melt, sea levels might rise 200 feet. In Antarctica, winds can blow at better than 200 mph, and temperatures drop as low as minus 128.6°F. There is not a single village or town, not a tree, bush, or blade of grass on the entire continent.

[6] But far from being merely a useless continent, Antarctica is vital to life on Earth. The continent's vast ice fields reflect sunlight back into space, preventing the planet from overheating. The cold water that the breakaway icebergs generate flows north and mixes with equatorial warm water, producing currents, clouds, and ultimately creating complex weather patterns. Antarctic seas teem with life, making them an important link in the world food chain. The frigid waters of the Southern Ocean are home to species of birds and mammals that are found nowhere else.

[7] The National Science Foundation (NSF) is the government agency responsible for the U.S. stations in Antarctica. Because of the continent's extreme cold and almost complete **isolation**, the NSF considers it to be the best place to study and understand such phenomena as temperature circulation in the oceans, unique animal life, ozone depletion, and glacial history. And buried deep in layers of Antarctic ice lie clues to ancient climates, clues such as trapped bubbles of atmospheric gases, which can help predict whether present and future global warming poses a real threat.

[8] Until scientists began the first serious study of the continent during the 1957–58 International Geophysical Year (IGY), a multicountry cooperative research project, Antarctica was **dismissed** as a vast, useless continent.

9   Based upon early explorations and questionable land grants, seven countries, including Great Britain, Chile, and Argentina, claim sovereignty over vast tracts of the continent. However, as IGY wound down, the question of who owns Antarctica came to a head. The 12 participating countries reached an international agreement, the Antarctic Treaty, which took effect in June 1961. The number has since grown, making 39 in all. It established Antarctica as a "continent for science and peace," and temporarily set aside all claims of sovereignty for as long as the treaty remains in effect.

10   The rules of the treaty meant that as tourists to Antarctica, passengers on our cruise ship needed neither passports nor visas. Except for a handful of sites of special scientific interest, specially protected areas, and specially managed areas, there was nothing to restrict us from wandering anywhere we wanted.

11   **Primarily** because of its scientific and ecological importance, many scientists feel that Antarctica should be dedicated to research only. They feel that tourists should not be permitted to come. However, recent events have shown that the greatest future threat to Antarctica may not be tourism or scientific stations, but the worldwide thirst for oil and minerals. "The reason the Antarctic Treaty was **negotiated** and went through so quickly," geologist John Splettstoesser explains, "is that at the time, relatively few minerals were known to exist there."

12   By the early 1970s, however, there were some **indications** that there might be gas and oil in Antarctica. The treaty countries decided that no commercial companies would be permitted to explore for resources. The Madrid Protocol bans all exploration or commercial exploitation of natural resources on the continent for the next 50 years.

13   Like the Antarctic Treaty itself, the Madrid Protocol is **binding** only on the 39 treaty countries. There's nothing to stop non-treaty countries from establishing commercial bases anywhere on the continent and doing whatever they please.

14   Where do we go from here? So far, no non-treaty nation has expressed a serious interest in setting up for business in Antarctica. So far, none of the countries claiming sovereignty has moved to formally annex Antarctic territory.

15   So whose continent is Antarctica, anyway? Former Vice President Albert Gore best expresses the feelings of those of us who have fallen in love with this strange and spectacular land: "I think that it should be held in trust as a global ecological reserve for all the people of the world, not just in this generation, but later generations to come as well."

(949 words)

CHAPTER 10 Matters of Life and Death

1 In a new book, *A Miracle and a **Privilege***, Dr. Francis Moore, 81, of Harvard Medical School, discusses a lifetime of grappling with the issue of when to help a patient die. An excerpt:

2 Doctors of our generation are not newcomers to this question. Going back to my internship days, I can remember many patients in pain, sometimes in a coma or delirious, with late, hopeless cancer. For many of them, we wrote an order for heavy medication—morphine by the clock. This was not talked about openly and little was written about it. It was essential, not **controversial**.

3 The best way to bring the problem into focus is to describe two patients whom I cared for. The first, **formerly** a nurse, had sustained a fractured pelvis in an automobile accident. A few days later her lungs seemed to fill up; her urine stopped; her heart developed dangerous rhythm disturbances. So there she was: in a coma, on dialysis, on a breathing machine, her heartbeat maintained with an electrical device. One day after rounds, my secretary said the husband and son of the patient wanted to see me. They told me their wife and mother was obviously going to die; she was a nurse and had told her family that she never wanted this kind of terrible death, being maintained by machines. I told them that while I respected their view, there was nothing intrinsically lethal about her situation. The kidney failure she had was just the kind for which the **artificial** kidney was most effective. While possibly a bit reassured, they were disappointed. Here was the head **surgeon**, seemingly determined to keep everybody alive, no matter what.

4 When patients start to get very sick, they often seem to fall apart all at once. The **reverse** is also true. Within a few days, the patient's pacemaker could be removed, and she awoke from her coma. About six months later I was again in my office. The door opened and in walked a gloriously fit woman. After some cheery words of **appreciation**, the father and son asked to speak to me alone. As soon as the door closed, both men became quite tearful. All that came out was, "We want you to know how wrong we were."

5 The second patient was an 85-year-old lady whose hair caught fire while she was smoking. She arrived with a deep burn; I knew it would surely be **fatal**. As a remarkable **coincidence**, there was a seminar going on at the time in medical ethics, given by the wife of an official of our university. She asked me if I had any sort of ethical problem I could bring up for discussion. I described the case and asked the students their opinion. After the discussion, I made a remark that was, in retrospect, a serious mistake. I said, "I'll take the word back to the nurses about her, and we will talk about it some more before we decide." The instructor and the students were shocked: "You mean this is a real patient?" The teacher of ethics was not accustomed to being challenged by reality. In any event, I went back and met with the nurses. A day or two later, when she was making no progress and was suffering terribly, we began to back off treatment. When she complained of pain, we gave her plenty of morphine. A great plenty. Soon she died quietly and not in pain. As a **reasonable** physician, you had better move ahead and do what you would want done for you. And do not discuss it with the world first. There is a lesson here for everybody. Assisting people to leave this life requires strong judgment and long experience to avoid its misuse.

(624 words)

CHAPTER 11 Switched at Birth: Women Learn the Truth 56 Years Later

1. When Oregon nurses handed Marjorie Angell her newborn daughter in the hospital in 1953, she insisted they had given her the wrong child. Her concerns were brushed off, but in an unlikely story that was 56 years in the making, her mother's **intuition** foreshadowed what was to come.

2. It was true. Her daughter had been switched at birth when she and the other baby were being bathed, but Marjorie Angell would never learn the truth because she died before it was revealed. "It's sad," DeeAnn Angell Schafer told "Good Morning America." "Just to think I missed out on knowing my own parents." Even though Kay Rene Reed Qualls said she enjoyed a wonderful life, she still feels guilty about the memories that should belong to DeeAnn and her family. "I look at them and I feel like I **cheated** somebody," she said. The story of two women who grew up in the wrong families just came to light last month to the surprise of everyone and no one.

A Secret Switch?

3. On May 3, 1953, DeeAnn Angell of Fossil, Oregon, and Kay Rene Reed of Condon, Oregon, were born at Pioneer Memorial Hospital in the eastern Oregon town of Heppner. They grew up, got married, and had children and grandchildren of their own. The women's lives were **uneventful** until last summer, when Kay Rene's brother, Bobby Reed, received a call from an 86-year-old woman who claimed to hold an astonishing secret. He met the woman in her nursing home. She said she had known the Reeds' mother and had lived next door to the Angell family in Fossil. Her shocking claim was that Kay Rene was not really a Reed at all; she was an Angell. The elderly woman said Kay Rene and DeeAnn were switched at birth. To bolster her story, she showed Bobby Reed an old photo of DeeAnn's sister. Reed saw an instant and **undeniable** resemblance to the woman raised as his sister.

Switched at Birth: Uncovering the Truth

4. If what the elderly woman said was correct, then DeeAnn really was Reed's sister and not Kay Rene. The secret stunned Reed, who was unsure what to do with the potential bombshell. He always had known and loved Kay Rene as his sister. Though Kay Rene was a brunette in a sea of blonds, no one ever thought to question her paternity.

5. Reed did not want anything to change, nor did he want to hurt anyone. He decided to tell his two oldest sisters, and one of them broke the news to Kay Rene. With both the Reed parents and the Angell parents dead, the children had to come together to uncover the truth about the **alleged** mix-up.

6. The families learned rumors of babies being switched at birth had been around for decades. In fact, Kay Rene first learned of such gossip in 1995 when her sister Carol told her during their dying father's last camping trip. After his death, Kay Rene's mother approached her about the subject. She acknowledged that she heard another new mother in the same hospital, where she had given birth, question if her baby was her own. But after looking into

Kay Rene's big brown eyes, she determined this was her baby and she would not bring the issue up anymore.

Growing Up with Questions

[7] Growing up, Kay Rene had questioned whether she truly was a Reed. She had her suspicions. She knew she did not look like anyone else in her family. Eventually, Kay Rene said, the rumors started in her family that maybe she was not really related to them.

"I think all the older sisters knew this," she said. But neither woman ever had blood tests and DNA testing was not an option.

[8] The doubts just lingered. Even Kay Rene's husband joked about whether the Reeds truly were her relatives after seeing her at family functions. Kay Rene just knew she did not want those thoughts to be true. She chalked them up to being ornery. She justified her placement in the Reed **clan** by saying her blue eyes came from her father. DeeAnn, too, had **suspicions** growing up. She wondered why she loved horses so much. She received a phone call from her sister in February to tell her about the news—the rumors might be true.

'Swisters': Switched Sisters

[9] Kay Rene wanted to know the truth; she needed to know it. So last month, she, her brother and their sister Dorothy met the blond-haired DeeAnn at a Kennewick, Washington, clinic for a DNA test. When Kay Rene finally met the Angell family, she realized she looked more like them. The DNA test confirmed what Kay Rene had seen with her own eyes and what DeeAnn realized the second she met Kay Rene. Kay Rene was not a Reed and had no **biological** link to her brother Bobby Reed. DeeAnn actually was Bobby Reed's sister and Kay Rene really was an Angell.

[10] The news was shocking and disturbing for Kay Rene, who felt as if she had lived a lie. She questioned if her memories actually belonged to her since she lived what should have been DeeAnn's life. DeeAnn finally got the answer to why she had an affinity for horses. Her biological father had been a horse trainer. DeeAnn and Kay Rene have become close following the **revelation**. They refer to each other as swisters, short for switched sisters.

[11] The hospital where the women were born has offered them counseling, but neither has accepted the offer. "We're old women now," Kay Rene said. They also have not decided if they will **sue** the facility. And while DeeAnn harbors at least some anger about the situation, Kay Rene said she does not because there is no use in it.

(960 words)

CHAPTER 12 Saving Her Sister's Life

*In 1990, Marissa Ayala's birth **stirred** a national debate—should families **conceive** one child to save another's life? In her own words, 18-year-old Marissa shares her story.*

My sister, Anissa, is like my second mom. Even though she is 18 years older than me, I do not know how much closer you could be with someone. In 1988, when she was 16, Anissa was **diagnosed** with leukemia. If she did not find a bone marrow **donor**, doctors said, she would die within three to five years. My parents were not matches, so for a few years they went through every organization they could—the Life-Savers Foundation of America, the National Marrow Donor Program, City of Hope—to find donors. They could not find a single match. At the time, the Hispanic rating for the National Marrow Donor Program was **practically** nonexistent, which means there were hardly any Hispanics on the list as donors. Since that's our **heritage**, it was not likely my parents would find someone who could work as a match for my sister.

Because matches are more common within families than with nonrelatives, every single extended family member got tested, but none of them matched with Anissa. Finally, one of my mom's best friends said as a joke, "Mary, you should have another baby." My mom, who was 43 at the time, thought her friend was crazy. But one night my mom dreamed that God was telling her to have a baby. She took that as a sign, and in April 1990 I was born. My parents were hoping I would be a match.

When I was old enough to be tested, I turned out to be a perfect match for my sister. My family was really excited and had me donate bone marrow to her 14 months after I was born—my marrow was transplanted into hers to **stimulate** healthy blood-cell growth. It was a total success. I recovered perfectly—my parents even have a video of me running around the same day I had my surgery. Although at first my sister had to be in an isolation room for a while so that no germs could get to her, she recovered well. She has been cancer-free for the past 18 years.

There has always been a lot of media attention surrounding our family because of our situation, though. It was apparently really controversial that my parents were having a baby just to save their other daughter's life. I do not remember a lot of that, because I was so much younger. When I was a baby, Anissa and I were on the cover of *Time* and there was a made-for-TV movie on NBC in 1993 called *For the Love of My Child: The Anissa Ayala Story*, made about my family's experience.

I first started really researching my own story when I was in the seventh grade. My friends were Googling themselves and nothing came up, but when I searched for myself a lot of news articles popped up. I read negative comments from a few newspapers about how my parents were just using me to save my sister's life and were not going to love me, and that what they did was morally wrong. It surprised me. I thought, "Really? People think about my family like that?" Some of the articles said that if I had not been a perfect match for my sister, my parents would have disowned me. And that just was not the case.

I try to see both sides of the story, but I ultimately do not agree with the **critics**. They were probably just looking out for my safety, thinking that my parents were going to have a baby

solely for the purpose of saving their child. But they do not know us **personally**: My family loves me so much.

8. Every year our family takes part in the Relay for Life cancer walk and we raise money for the American Cancer Society. We try to spread the message that the need for marrow donors is great. And more important, that despite being diagnosed with whatever type of cancer, there is a way to get through it.

9. There are so many ways growing up as "the baby who saved her sister" has influenced my life. I have taken it, been humbled by it, and have grown from it. But it will not be my whole life story. In the future, I plan to study either child development or psychology. My dad always tells me, "Marissa, you should do something you want to do every day." I want to help people.

(768 words)

APPENDIX 2　WORD LIST

このリストには、本書のReading Analysis本文で使われている重要語句とその初出ページを収録しています。ただし、固有名詞は除外しています。

※Vocabularyで取り上げている語句は太字で示し、NOTESで取り上げている語句はページ番号のあとにNを付けています。

A

a sea of	105 N
accredited	76 N
accumulation	42 N
acknowledge	22
acquaintance	55
adolescence	41 N
affinity	107 N
agriculture	68
alleged	105
alumnus	71 N
ancestry	80 N
anchor	75 N
annex	90 N
antelope	80 N
anthill	75 N
application	68
appreciate	23
appreciation	96
artificial	96
attribute	85 N
austral	78 N
autonomy	52

B

bag on	41 N
battering	41 N
be accustomed to	98 N
be predisposed to	41 N
beneficial	51
binding	90
bio-acoustician	76 N
biodegradable	70 N
biological	107
black-foot ferret	80 N
blade	86 N
blood-cell	112 N
blossom	44 N
bolster	104 N
bombshell	105 N
bone marrow	111 N
boredom	78 N
born digital	32 N
bottom out	44 N

bring ... up	105 N
brunette	105 N
brush off	103 N
buoyant	41 N
by the clock	95 N

C

cacophony	76 N
candy heart	35 N
capable	14
captive	75 N
cascade	78 N
Caucasian	42 N
certainty	15
chalk up	106 N
chaos	44
chasm	32 N
cheat	103
cheery	96 N
choreograph	62 N
clan	106
clerical	53 N
coalition	30 N
coincide	44
coincidence	98
coma	95 N
competence	16
compose	62
compost	67 N
conceive	111
condor	80 N
confine	78
contemporary	60
contend	85 N
continuity	44
controversial	95
coronary	53 N
counterrevolutionary	29 N
cozy up to	80 N
Cretaceous	76 N
critic	112
crocus	30 N
crucial	78
crumble	42 N

143

cue	76 N
curator	75 N
cyber age	29 N

D

dainty	78 N
dedicate	89 N
deep burn	98 N
delightful	22
delirious	95 N
delve into	29 N
demographer	15 N
deprive	85
descent	42 N
deserving	14
destiny	16 N
developmental psychologist	59 N
developmentally	35 N
devoid of	30 N
diagnose	111
dialysis	96 N
digital divide	32 N
dilute	15 N
discourage	14
dismiss	87
disown	112 N
disproportionate	14 N
dissect	29 N
donor	111
draft	70
due to	62
dumb	22 N
dwindle	80 N

E

ecological	89 N
elaborate	25
emanate	76 N
embrace	30
enable ... to *do*	62 N
enigmatic	44 N
enlightened	69
ensure	80
enthusiast	30
epidemiologist	51 N
equatorial	87 N
eschew	34 N
ethical	98 N
ethics	98 N
exception	30
excerpt	95 N

exhibit	76
expectancy	49 N
expertise	59
exploitation	85 N
extinct	80 N

F

fabulous	85 N
facilitate	32
fact of life	32 N
fallacy	49 N
fare	42 N
fatal	98
feathered	76 N
feedback	42
fell	75 N
fiercely	80 N
folk wisdom	13 N
forage	78 N
foreshadow	103 N
formerly	96
fractured pelvis	96 N
fraught with	41 N
frigid	87 N
function	106 N
furry	76 N

G

generous	25
geologist	89 N
germ	112 N
gerontology	53 N
gibbon	76 N
glacial	87 N
gloriously	96 N
golden lion tamarin	80 N
gospel	81 N
graceful	80 N
grapple with	95 N
grudging	30 N
guardian	30 N
gunite	78 N

H

habitat	76
handout	75 N
harbor	107 N
harem	78 N
headline	60 N
heady	41 N
heed	80 N

WORD LIST

heredity	49 N
heritage	111
hoot	76 N
hormonal	41 N
hornbill	76 N
horse-drawn	70 N
howl	76 N
humble	114 N
hypothesis	54

I

icecap	86 N
immerse	76 N
immersion	80 N
immune	53
immune system	53 N
in retrospect	98 N
in trust	90 N
inbreeding	80 N
incompatibility	23 N
incorrect	13 N
indication	89
induce	76 (N)
inhospitable	86 N
insulting	22
integrate	32
intensify	75 N
intensive	68
intimate	35 N
intricate	80 N
intrinsic	41 N
intrinsically	96 N
intuition	103
invest	60
irresistible	85 N
isolation	87

J

jeopardize	85 N
jeopardy	44 N

K

kidney failure	96 N
kindle	30 N

L

land grant	89 N
landmark	50
lapsed	21 N
launch	41
leggy	78 N

lethal	96 N
lethargy	76 N
leukemia	111 N
lifespan	41 N
liken ... to	41 N
linger	106 N
longevity	49
lure	85 N
lush	76 N
lyrics	62 N

M

macaque	78 N
manipulate	75 N
matchmaking	24 N
mediated	34 N
menagerie	75 N
merge ... into	78 N
mimic	78 N
misuse	98 N
mix-up	105 N
moderately	50 N
morally	112 N
moratorium	30 N
morphine	95 N
motivation	15

N

negotiate	88
newcomer	95 N
nocturnal	76 N
nonexistent	111 N
nonprofit	71 N
nonrelative	111 N
note	59 N
nursing home	104 N

O

oblige	80
obsession	59
offspring	78 N
omnipotence	44 N
on the cutting edge of	30 N
on the side	70 N
organic	68
ornery	106 N
oryx	80 N
outgoing	15 N
outperform	30
overall	42
overhaul	78 N

oversee	35
ozone depletion	87 N

P

pacemaker	96 N
pachyderm	78 N
parlance	80 N
paternity	105 N
peril	41 N
persistence	24
personally	112
physician	98 N
platypus	76 N
plow	68
plummet	44 N
plunge	41
plunk	35 N
pollute	85 N
practically	111
prairie-dog	80 N
prestigious	60
primarily	88
primate	80 N
privilege	95
prodigy	59 N
profound	50
profoundly	29 N
proliferate	80 N
promote	14
prompt	78
prophecy	14 N
put ... into practice	68 N

Q

quit	59

R

rage	59
rarity	75 N
reasonable	98
regional	68
relative	21
relevant to	32
religious	21
reluctantly	23
remote	85
reproduce	75
reserves	85 N
revelation	107
reverse	96
rhino	78 N

rhythm disturbance	96 N
rivalry	14 N
roam	78 N
romp	76 N
round	96 N
ruin	85

S

satisfaction	52
savanna	76 N
scamper	78 N
scoop out	75 N
self-approval	41 N
self-doubt	41 N
self-esteem	16
selfish	13 N
self-regard	41 N
sheet music	59 N
shin	70 N
shriek	76 N
sibling	14 N
similarity	42
sire	78 N
situational	42 N
slighted	60 N
snicker	22 N
socioeconomic	54 N
solar shower	70 N
solely	112
son-in-law	22 N
sound	55 N
sovereignty	89 N
spearhead	42 N
spectrum	30 N
spinsterhood	25 N
stab	23 N
standardized test	30 N
stimulate	112
stir	111
strive	76
studbook	80 N
stuffy	68 N
stun	105 N
suburban	71
sue	107
sullen	44 N
superficial	42 N
support *one*self	70 N
supportive	15
suppress	53
surgeon	96

surreptitiously	75 N
suspicion	106
sustain	96 N
sustainable	68
switch	104 N

T

take effect	89 N
teem with	87 N
thirst	89 N
throe	41 N
tract	89 N
transition	42
transplant	112 N
treasure	85
trill	76 N
tundra	80 N
turmoil	42 N

U

ultimately	87 N
undaunted	24 N
undeniable	104
undermine	60
uneventful	104
unparalleled	85 N
uproar	21 N
upswing	44 N
urine	96 N

V

veld	78 N
verbal	15
vibraphonist	62 N
virtually	30
vital	34
vulnerable	44

W

warfare	41 N
weed vegetable bed	67 N
well-adjusted	15 N
well-being	44 N
wind down	89 N
window dressing	32 N
work ethic	60 N

Text Credits:

Chapter 1: Copyright 1990 by Alfie Kohn. Reprinted from *Health* magazine with the author's permission.

Chapter 2: By Marian Hyun, *Newsday*. Marian Hyun is a former writer who runs a nonprofit organization, Jazz Choreography Enterprises.

Chapter 3: By Victoria Irwin, *The Christian Science Monitor*. Originally published in the Christian Science Monitor, March 11, 2003. Reprinted with permission of author.

Chapter 4: Reprinted with permission of Scripps Howard News Service.

Chapter 5: Reprinted with the permission of Patricia Skalka.

Chapter 6: Excerpts about Wolfgang Amadeus Mozart and William James Sidis, from "10 Amazing Child Prodigies Across Time." Reprinted with permission by Kathryn Vercillo; Excerpt about Kim Ung-Yong from "10 Extraordinary Child Prodigies." From Oddee.com.

Chapter 7: Used with the permission of The Associated Press © 2009. All rights reserved.

Chapter 8: From Newsweek, July 17, 1989 © 1989 IBT Media. All rights reserved. Used by permission and protected by the Copyright Laws of the United States. The printing, copying, redistribution, or retransmission of this Content without express written permission is prohibited.

Chapter 9: Originally published in *Popular Science* 21 no. 1 (January, 1992) Daniel and Sally Grotta. Printed with permission of the authors.

Chapter 11: Reprinted by permission. ABC News—Good Morning America.

Chapter 12: Copyright © 2009 Conde Nast Publications. All rights reserved. Originally published in Teen Vogue. Reprinted by permission.

教師用音声CD有り（非売品）

Reading Dynamics — Skills for Academic Success
思考力を高めるためのリーディングスキル

2016年3月1日　初版発行
2020年1月20日　第 4 刷

編著者　山科美和子、横山三鶴、沖野泰子
発行者　松村達生
発行所　センゲージ ラーニング株式会社
　　　　〒102-0073　東京都千代田区九段北1-11-11　第2フナトビル5階
　　　　電話 03-3511-4392　FAX 03-3511-4391
　　　　e-mail: elt@cengagejapan.com
　　　　copyright©2016 センゲージ ラーニング株式会社

装　丁　　足立友幸（parastyle）
編集協力　飯尾緑子（parastyle）
印刷・製本　株式会社平河工業社

ISBN 978-4-86312-287-1

もし落丁、乱丁、その他不良品がありましたら、お取り替えいたします。本書の全部または一部を無断で複写（コピー）することは、著作権法上での例外を除き、禁じられていますのでご注意ください。